Configuring Advanced Windows Server® 2012 Services R2 Exam 70-412

Lab Manual

Patrick Regan

WILEY

SENIOR EXECUTIVE EDITOR	Bryan Gambrel
EDITORIAL ASSISTANT	Jessy Moor
EXECUTIVE MARKETING MANAGER	Dan Sayre
ASSOCIATE PRODUCTION MANAGER	Joyce Poh

www.wiley.com/college/microsoft or
call the MOAC Toll-Free Number: 888-764-7001 (U.S. & Canada only)

ISBN 978-1-118-88302-0

Printed in the United States of America

BRIEF CONTENTS

CONTENTS

LAB 1
CONFIGURING NETWORK LOAD BALANCING

THIS LAB CONTAINS THE FOLLOWING EXERCISES AND ACTIVITIES:

BEFORE YOU BEGIN

The lab environment consists of student workstations connected to a local area network, along with a server that functions as the domain controller for a domain called contoso.com. The computers required for this lab are listed in Table 1-1.

Table 1-1
Computers required for Lab 1

Computer	Operating System	Computer Name
Server (VM 1)	Windows Server 2012 R2	RWDC01
Server (VM 2)	Windows Server 2012 R2	Server01
Server (VM 3)	Windows Server 2012 R2	Server02
Server (VM 4)	Windows Server 2012 R2	Storage01

In addition to the computers, you will also require the software listed in Table 1-2 to complete Lab 1.

Table 1-2
Software required for Lab 1

Software	Location
Lab 1 student worksheet	Lab1_worksheet.docx (provided by instructor)

Working with Lab Worksheets

Each lab in this manual requires that you answer questions, shoot screen shots, and perform other activities that you will document in a worksheet named for the lab, such as Lab01_worksheet.docx. You will find these worksheets on the book companion site. It is recommended that you use a USB flash drive to store your worksheets, so you can submit them to your instructor for review. As you perform the exercises in each lab, open the appropriate worksheet file, fill in the required information, and save the file to your flash drive.

After completing this lab, you will be able to:

■ Install and configure NLB

■ Create and configure a NLB cluster

■ Configure DNS

■ Configure cluster properties

■ Manage the cluster nodes

Estimated lab time: 85 minutes

Exercise 1.1	Installing Network Load Balancing
Overview	In this exercise, you will install the Network Load Balancing Feature on two Windows Server 2012 R2 servers.
Mindset	The company website must be fault tolerant, so you decide to use Network Load Balancing. What is required to implement Network Load Balancing?
Completion time	25 minutes

1. Log into Server01 as **contoso\administrator** with the password of **P@$$w0rd**.

2. On Server01, right-click the **Network Status** icon on the Taskbar and choose **Open Network and Sharing Center**.

3. When the Network and Sharing Center opens (as shown in Figure 1-1), click the second Ethernet connection.

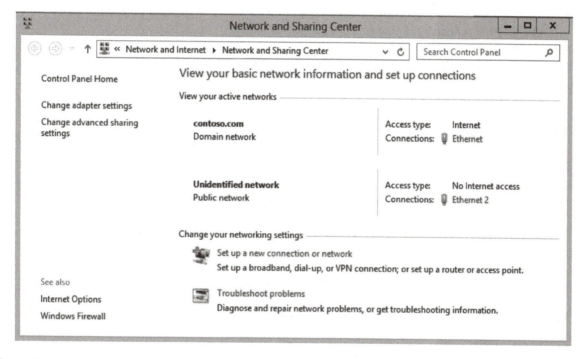

Figure 1-1
Managing network settings

4. When the Ethernet 2 Status dialog box opens, click **Properties**. The Ethernet Properties dialog box opens.

5. Double-click **Internet Protocol Version 4 (TCP/IPv4)**. The Internet Protocol Version 4 (TCP/IPv4) Properties dialog box.

6. Configure the following settings and then click **OK**:

   IP address: **192.168.1.61**

   Subnet mask: **255.255.255.0**

7. Click **OK** to close the Ethernet Properties dialog box.

8. Click **Close** to close the Ethernet Status. Close Network and Sharing Center.

9. Log into Server02 as **contoso\administrator** with the password of **P@$$w0rd**. Right-click the Network Status icon in the Taskbar and choose **Open Network and Sharing Center**.

10. When the Network and Sharing Center opens, click the second Ethernet connection.

11. When the Ethernet Status dialog box opens, click **Properties**. The Ethernet Properties dialog box opens.

12. Double-click **Internet Protocol Version 4 (TCP/IPv4)**. The Internet Protocol Version 4 (TCP/IPv4) Properties dialog box opens.

13. Configure the following settings and then click **OK**:

    IP address: **192.168.1.71**

    Subnet mask: **255.255.255.0**

14. Click **OK** to close the Ethernet 2 Properties dialog box.

15. Click **Close** to close the Ethernet 2 Status. Close **Network and Sharing Center**.

16. On Server01, using the **Server Manager** console, click **Manage > Add Roles and Features**.

17. When the Add Roles and Features Wizard starts, click **Next**.

18. On the Select installation type page, click **Next**.

19. On the Select destination server page, click **Next**.

20. On the Select server roles page, click **Next**.

21. On the Select features page, click to select the **Network Load Balancing**. When it asks you to add features required for NLB, click **Add Features**. Click **Next**.

22. On the Confirm installation selections page, click **Install**.

23. When the installation is complete, click **Close**.

24. Using the same procedure that you used for Server01, install the Network Loading Balancing feature on Server02.

End of exercise. Leave the Server Manager open for the next exercise.

Exercise 1.2	Creating an NLB Cluster
Overview	In this exercise, you will create the NLB Cluster using Server01 and Server02.
Mindset	
Completion time	15 minutes

Adding the First Node

1. On Server01, using **Server Manager**, click **Tools > Network Load Balancing Manager**. The Network Load Balancing Manager opens.

2. Right-click **Network Load Balancing Clusters** and choose **New Cluster**, as shown in Figure 1-2. The New Cluster: Connect Wizard opens.

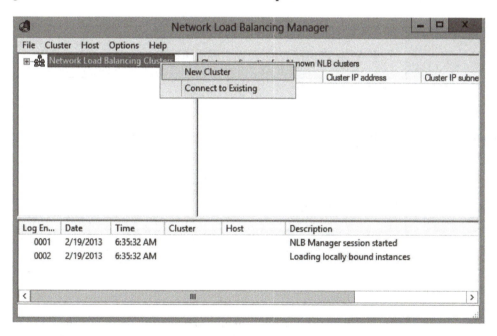

Figure 1-2
Creating a new NLB cluster

3. In the Host text box, type **Server01** and then click **Connect**.

4. The interface hosts the virtual IP address and receives the client traffic to load balance. Click the second Ethernet interface and then click **Next**.

5. On the Host parameters page, select a value in the Priority (unique host identifier) drop-down list.

Question 1	*What is the default priority?*

6. In the Dedicated IP addresses section, verify that the dedicated IP address from the chosen interface is visible in the list and then click **Next**.

7. On the New Cluster: Cluster IP Addresses page, click **Add**. The Add IP Address dialog box opens.

8. Type the following information and then click **OK**.

   IPv4 address: **192.168.1.65**

   Subnet mask: **255.255.255.0**

9. Back at the New Cluster: Cluster IP Addresses page, click **Next**.

10. On the New Cluster: Cluster Parameters page, type **web.contoso.com** in the Full Internet name text box.

Question 2	*What is the default cluster operation mode?*

11. Click **Next**.

12. On the New Cluster: Port Rules page, click **Edit** to open the Add/Edit Port Rule dialog box.

Question 3	*What is the filtering mode set to?*

13. Click **OK** to close the Add/Edit Port Rule.

14. Click **Finish**.

15. Take a screen shot of the Network Load Balancing Manager by pressing Alt+Prt Scr and then paste it into your Lab 1worksheet file in the page provided by pressing Ctrl+V.

Adding the Second Node

1. On Server01, using Network Load Balancing Manager, right-click **web.contoso.com** and choose **Add Host to Cluster**.

2. When the Add Host to Cluster dialog box opens, type **server02** and then click **Connect**.

3. When the interfaces are displayed, click the second Ethernet interface, and then click **Next**.

4. On the Add Host to Cluster: Host Parameters page, click **Next**.

5. On the Add Host to Cluster: Port Rules page, click **Finish**.

6. Watch Network Load Balancing Manager until both nodes are converged. You may need press **F5** to refresh the console.

7. Take a screen shot of the Network Load Balancing Manager by pressing Alt+Prt Scr and then paste it into your Lab 1 worksheet file in the page provided by pressing Ctrl+V.

End of exercise. Keep the Network Load Balancing Manager open for later exercises.

Exercise 1.3	Configuring DNS
Overview	In this exercise, you will configure DNS resource records.
Mindset	There are two things still missing. First, you will need to install IIS, and deploy the websites on Server01 and Server02. So when you are ready to go live, what are the last steps needed so that users can reach the websites?
Completion time	10 minutes

1. Log into RWDC01 as **contoso\administrator** with the password of **P@$$w0rd**.

2. When Server Manager opens, click **Tools > DNS**.

3. When the DNS Manager console opens, expand **RWDC01**, expand **Forward Lookup Zones**, and then click **contoso.com**.

4. Right-click **contoso.com** and choose **New Host (A or AAAA)**.

5. When the New Host dialog box opens, enter the following:

   Name: **web**

   IP address: **192.168.1.65**

6. Click to select **Create associated pointer (PTR) record**, and click **Add Host**.

7. Click OK and then click **Done** to close the New Host dialog box.

8. Right-click **contoso.com** and choose **New Alias (CNAME)**.

9. When the New Resource Record dialog box opens, type the following and then click **OK**:

   Alias name: **www**

Fully qualified domain name (FQDN) for target host: **web.contoso.com**

10. Click **OK** then close the DNS Manager console.

End of exercise. Close the DNS Manager.

Exercise 1.4	Configuring Cluster Properties
Overview	In this exercise, you will redefine the port rules for only the ports that you need.
Mindset	As mentioned earlier, the cluster is meant to support a website. What ports will you need to support the websites?
Completion time	10 minutes

1. On Server01, using Network Load Balancing Manager, right-click **web.contoso.com** and choose **Cluster Properties**.

2. When the Web.contoso.com Properties dialog box opens, click the **Port Rules** tab. The Port Rules tab is shown in Figure 1-3.

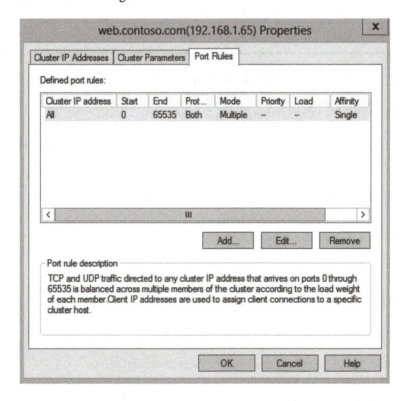

Figure 1-3
Configuring cluster parameters

3. Click the current rule and click **Remove**.

4. Click **Add**. The Add/Edit Port Rule dialog box opens.

Question 4	What filtering mode is selected and what affinity is selected?

Question 5	Why would you need to use single affinity?

5. Change the protocols to **TCP**.

6. Change the port range to the following and then click **OK**:

   From: **80**

   To: **80**

7. Click **Add**. The Add/Edit Port Rule dialog box opens.

8. Change the protocols to **TCP**.

9. Change the port range to the following and then click **OK**:

   From: **443**

   To: **443**

10. Click **OK** to close the Properties dialog box.

11. Watch Network Load Balancing Manager until both nodes are converged. You may need to press **F5** to refresh the console.

End of exercise. Keep the Load Balancing Manager open for the next exercise.

Exercise 1.5	Managing Cluster Nodes
Overview	In this exercise, you will manage cluster nodes.
Mindset	You need to do maintenance on the nodes. At this time, you need to stop one of the nodes, and then bring the node back online.
Completion time	5 minutes

1. On Server01, using Network Load Balancing Manager, right-click **SERVER01** and choose **Control Host > Drainstop**.

Question 6	What does drainstop do?

2. Take a screen shot of the Network Load Balancing Manager by pressing Alt+Prt Scr and then paste it into your Lab 1 worksheet file in the page provided by pressing Ctrl+V.

3. Click **web.contoso.com**.

Question 7	What is the status of the Server01 node?

4. Right-click **Server01** and choose **Control Host > Start**.

5. Right-click **Server01** and choose **Control Host > Stop**.

6. Right-click **Server01** and choose **Control Host > Start**.

7. Watch Network Load Balancing Manager until both nodes are Enabled. You may need to press **F5** to refresh the console.

End of exercise. Leave the Network Load Balancing Manager open for the next exercise.

Exercise 1.6	Removing an NLB Cluster
Overview	In the first part of this exercise, you will delete the cluster. In the second part, you will remove NLB so that it will not interfere with future lessons.
Mindset	
Completion time	5 minutes

1. On Server01, using Network Load Balancing Manager, right-click **web.contoso.com** and choose **Delete Cluster**. Click **Yes** to remove NLB.

2. Close **Network Load Balancing Manager**.

3. Using **Server Manager**, click **Manage**, and then click **Remove Roles and Features**.

4. When the Remove Roles and Features Wizard opens, click **Next**.

5. On the Select destination server page, click **Next**.

6. On the Remove server roles page, click **Next**.

7. On the Remove features page, click to deselect **Network Load Balancing**.

8. When a dialog box as you to remove features, click **Remove Features**.

9. Back on the Remove features page, click **Next**.

10. On the Confirm removal selections page, click **Remove**.

11. When the feature is removed, click **Close**.

12. Reboot Server01.

13. Go to Server02 and repeat the process in steps 3 through 11 to remove its Network Load Balancing feature.

14. Reboot Server02.

End of exercise. Close any open windows before you begin the next exercise.

LAB REVIEW QUESTIONS

Completion time   10 minutes

1. In Exercise 1.1, when you installed NLB, was it a role or was it a feature?

2. In Exercise 1.2, which mode (multicast or unicast) should be used when you have two network cards?

3. In Exercise 1.2, if you use multicast mode, which MAC addresses are assigned to the NLB network adapter?

4. In Exercise 1.3, what is the advantage of using an alias resource record?

5. In Exercise 1.4, which filter mode should be selected when you want one server to be the primary web server and the other node to wait until the primary server goes down?

6. In Exercise 1.5, what occurs when you do not use drainstop to stop a node?

Lab Challenge	Upgrading an NLB Cluster
Overview	To complete this challenge, you will describe how to add drivers to a Windows image by writing the high-level steps of processing network policies.
Mindset	An NLB cluster is running on two servers running Windows Server 2008 R2. What would you do to upgrade the cluster to Windows Server 2012 R2?
Completion time	10 minutes

End of lab. You can log off or start a different lab. If you want to restart this lab, you'll need to click the End Lab button in order for the lab to be reset.

LAB 2
CONFIGURING FAILOVER CLUSTERING

THIS LAB CONTAINS THE FOLLOWING EXERCISES AND ACTIVITIES:

Exercise 2.1   Configuring the iSCSI Client

Exercise 2.2   Installing Failover Clustering

Exercise 2.3   Creating a Failover Cluster

Exercise 2.4   Configuring the Quorum

Exercise 2.5   Configuring a Clustered Storage Space

Exercise 2.6   Implementing Cluster Aware Updating

Lab Challenge   Upgrading a Failover Cluster

BEFORE YOU BEGIN

The lab environment consists of student workstations connected to a local area network, along with a server that functions as the domain controller for a domain called contoso.com. The computers required for this lab are listed in Table 2-1.

Table 2-1
Computers required for Lab 2

Computer	Operating System	Computer Name
Server (VM 1)	Windows Server 2012 R2	RWDC01
Server (VM 2)	Windows Server 2012 R2	Server01
Server (VM 3)	Windows Server 2012 R2	Server02
Server (VM 4)	Windows Server 2012 R2	Storage01

In addition to the computers, you will also require the software listed in Table 2-2 to complete Lab 2.

Table 2-2
Software required for Lab 2

Software	Location
Lab 2 student worksheet	Lab2_worksheet.docx (provided by instructor)

Working with Lab Worksheets

Each lab in this manual requires that you answer questions, shoot screen shots, and perform other activities that you will document in a worksheet named for the lab, such as Lab02_worksheet.docx. You will find these worksheets on the book companion site. It is recommended that you use a USB flash drive to store your worksheets, so you can submit them to your instructor for review. As you perform the exercises in each lab, open the appropriate worksheet file, fill in the required information, and save the file to your flash drive.

After completing this lab, you will be able to:

- Install and configure a failover cluster

- Configure quorum

- Implement Cluster Aware Updating

- Upgrade a cluster

Estimated lab time: 145 minutes

Exercise 2.1	Configuring the iSCSI Client
Overview	For a failover cluster to function, you need to have a shared drive. Storage01 is an iSCSI target, which has iSCSI drives that can be used by Server01 and Server02. In this exercise, you will connect to the iSCSI drives using the built-in iSCSI client software that comes with Windows Server 2012 R2.
Mindset	Why do failover cluster nodes need to connect to a SAN?
Completion time	25 minutes

1. Log into Server01 as **contoso\administrator** with the password of **Pa$$w0rd**. Server Manager opens.

2. With Server Manager, click **Tools > iSCSI Initiator**.

3. When a message indicates that the Microsoft iSCSI service is not running, click **Yes** to start it.

4. When the iSCSI Initiator Properties dialog box opens, type **storage01.contoso.com** in the Target: text box (as shown in Figure 2-1) and then click **Quick Connect**.

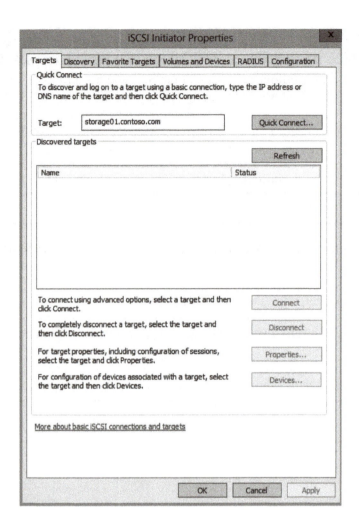

Figure 2-1
Using Quick Connect

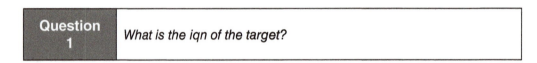

Question 1	*What is the iqn of the target?*

5. To close the Quick Connect dialog box, click **Done**.

6. Click **OK** to close to the iSCSI Initiator Properties dialog box.

7. Using Server Manager, click **Tools > Computer Management**.

8. When the Computer Management console opens, under the **Storage** node, click **Disk Management**.

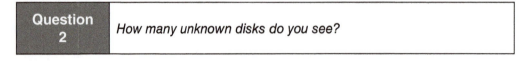

Question 2	*How many unknown disks do you see?*

9. Right-click **Disk 1** and choose **Online**.

10. Right-click **Disk 1** and choose **Initialize Disk**.

11. When the Initialize Disk dialog box opens, click **OK**.

12. Right-click the unallocated volume on Disk 1 and choose **New Simple Volume**.

13. When the New Simple Volume Wizard opens, click **Next**.

14. On the Specify Volume Size page, click **Next**.

15. On the Assign Drive Letter or Path page, click **Next**.

16. On the Format Partition, change the Volume Label to **SharedDisk**. Click **Next**.

17. When the new Simple Volume Wizard completes, click **Finish**.

18. Right-click the **Disk 2** and choose **Online**.

19. Right-click the **Disk 2** and choose **Initialize Disk**.

20. When the Initialize Disk dialog box opens, click **OK**.

21. Right-click the unallocated volume on Disk 2 and choose **New Simple Volume**.

22. When the New Simple Volume Wizard opens, click **Next**.

23. On the Specify Volume Size page, click **Next**.

24. On the Assign Drive Letter or Path page, click **Next**.

25. On the Format Partition, change the Volume Label to **QuorumDisk**. Click **Next**.

26. When the wizard is done, click **Finish**.

27. Take a screen shot of Computer Management by pressing Alt+Prt Scr and then paste it into your Lab 2 worksheet file in the page provided by pressing Ctrl+V.

28. Close **Computer Management**. If you have any dialog boxes to format a disk, click Cancel.

29. Log into Server02 as **contoso\administrator** with the password of **Pa$$w0rd**. Server Manager opens.

30. With Server Manager, click **Tools > iSCSI Initiator**.

31. When a message indicates the Microsoft iSCSI service is not running, click **Yes**.

32. When the iSCSI Initiator Properties dialog box opens, type **storage01.contoso.com** and then click **Quick Connect**.

35. On the Quick Connect dialog box, click **Done**.

33. Click the **Volumes and Devices** tab.

34. Click Auto Configure button.

35. Click **OK** to close to the iSCSI Initiator Properties dialog box.

End of exercise. You can leave the Server Manager open for the next exercise.

Exercise 2.2	Installing Failover Clustering
Overview	In this exercise, you will install Failover Clustering.
Mindset	
Completion time	15 minutes

1. On Server01, using the **Server Manager** console, click **Manage > Add Roles and Features**.

2. When the Add Roles and Features Wizard starts, click **Next**.

3. On the Select installation type page, click **Next**.

4. On the Select destination server page, click **Next**.

5. On the Select server roles page, click **Next**.

6. On the Select features page, click to select the **Failover Clustering.** When you are prompted to add features required for NLB, click **Add Features** and then click **Next**.

7. On the Confirm installation selections page, click **Install**.

8. When the installation is complete, click **Close**.

9. Using the same procedure that you used for Server01, install the Failover Clustering feature on Server02.

End of exercise. You can leave the Server Manager open for the next exercise.

Exercise 2.3	Creating a Failover Cluster
Overview	In this exercise, you will create a failover cluster using two virtual machines running Windows Server 2012 R2.
Mindset	What are the requirements to create a failover cluster using two servers?
Completion time	25 minutes

1. On Server01, right-click the **Network Status** icon on the Taskbar and choose **Open Network and Sharing Center**.

2. When the Network and Sharing Center dialog box open, click on the second Ethernet interface.

3. When the Ethernet 2 Status dialog box opens, click **Properties**.

4. Scroll down and double-click **Internet Protocol Version 4 (TCP/IPv4)**.

5. Configure the following and then click **OK**:

   IP address: **192.168.5.1**

   Subnet Mask: **255.255.255.0**

6. Click **OK** to close Ethernet Properties.

7. Click **Close** to close Ethernet Status.

8. Close **Network and Sharing Center**.

9. On Server02, right-click the Network Status icon and choose **Open Network and Sharing Center**.

10. When the Network and Sharing Center opens, click on the second Ethernet interface.

11. When the Ethernet Status dialog box opens, click **Properties**.

12. Scroll down and double-click **Internet Protocol Version 4 (TCP/IPv4)**.

13. Configuring the following and then click **OK**:

    IP address: **192.168.5.2**

    Subnet Mask: **255.255.255.0**

14. Click **OK** to close Ethernet 2 Properties.

15. Click **Close** to close Ethernet 2 Status.

16. Close **Network and Sharing Center**.

17. On Server01, using **Server Manager**, click **Tools > Failover Cluster Manager**. The Failover Cluster Manager console opens, as shown in Figure 2-2.

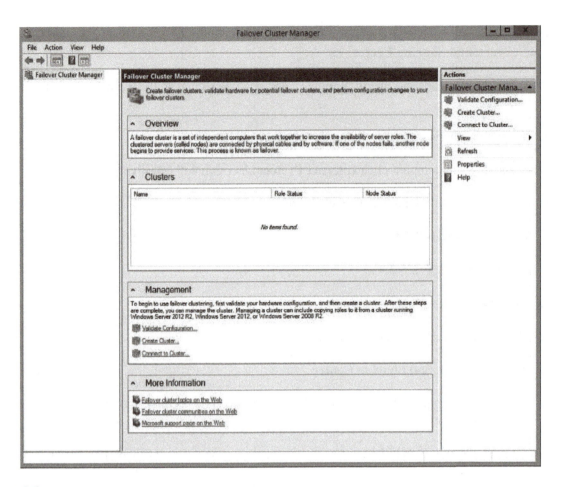

Figure 2-2
Opening the Failover Cluster Manager console

18. In the Actions pane, click **Validate Configuration**.

19. When the Validate a Configuration Wizard opens, click **Next**.

20. On the Select Servers or a Cluster page, type **Server01** in the Enter name text box and then click **Add**.

21. Type **Server02** in the Enter name text box. Click **Add** and then click **Next**.

22. On the Testing Options page, **Run all tests (recommended)** is already selected. Click **Next**.

23. On the Confirmation page, click **Next**.

24. When the Summary is done, scroll through to verify that everything passed.

Note:	*You will get two warnings: Validate IP Configuration and Validate network. This is caused by not having a usable adapter with a defined default gateway.*

25. Take a screen shot of the Validate a Configuration Wizard window by pressing Alt+Prt Scr and then paste it into your Lab 2 worksheet file in the page provided by pressing Ctrl+V.

26. Create the cluster now using the validated nodes already selected. Click **Finish**.

27. When the Create Cluster wizard opens, click **Next**.

28. On the Cluster Name, type **Cluster1**. In the Address column. Uncheck the check box next to 192.168.5.0/24.

29. Next to 192.168.1.0/24, click **Click here to type an address**, type **192.168.1.52**, and then click **Next**, as shown in Figure 2-3.

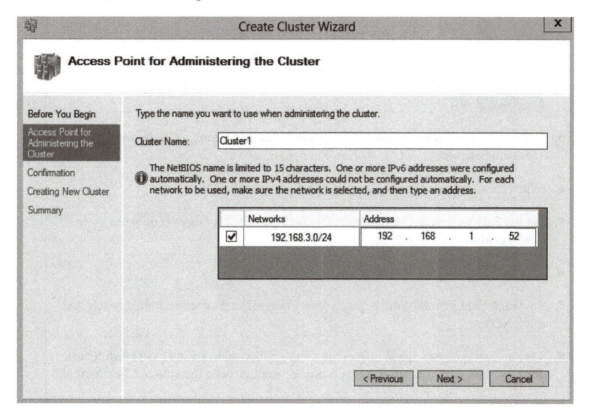

Figure 2-3
Specifying the cluster address

30. On the Confirmation page, Add all eligible storage to the cluster is already selected. Click **Next**.

31. When the wizard is completed, click **Finish**.

32. In the Failover Cluster Manager, expand **cluster1.contoso.com**.

33. Take a screen shot of the Failover Cluster Manager window by pressing Alt+Prt Scr and then paste it into your Lab 2 worksheet file in the page provided by pressing Ctrl+V.

End of exercise. You can leave the Failover Cluster Manager open for the next exercise.

Exercise 2.4	Configuring the Quorum
Overview	In this exercise, since you only have two nodes, you will create a quorum using a disk witness.
Mindset	When would you need to have a quorum when creating a failover cluster?
Completion time	10 minutes

1. On Server01, with Failover Cluster Manager, click the **Nodes** node. You should see Server01 and Server02.

2. Expand **Storage** and then click **Disks**.

Question 3	*What disks do you have and how are the disks assigned?*

3. Right-click **Cluster1.contoso.com** and choose **More Actions > Configure Cluster Quorum Settings**.

4. When the Configure Cluster Quorum Wizard opens, click **Next**.

5. On the Select Quorum Configuration Option page, click **Advanced quorum configuration** and click **Next**.

6. On the Select Voting Configuration page, click **Next**.

7. On the Select Quorum Witness page, With Configure a disk witness already selected, click **Next**.

8. On the Configure Storage Witness page, The smaller shared disk (2 GB) disk (Cluster Disk 2) is already selected. If is this is not apparent, expand the option. Click **Next**.

9. On the Confirmation page, click **Next**.

10. When the wizard is complete, click **Finish**.

11. Take a screen shot of the Failover Cluster Manager pressing Alt+Prt Scr and then paste it into your Lab 2 worksheet file in the page provided by pressing Ctrl+V.

End of exercise. Close any open windows before you begin the next exercise.

Exercise 2.5	Configuring a Clustered Storage Space
Overview	In this exercise, you will create a clustered storage space from three iSCSI drives.
Mindset	
Completion time	30 minutes

1. On Server01, using the **Server Manager** console, click **Manage > Add Roles and Features**.

2. When the Add Roles and Features Wizard opens, on the Before You Begin page, click **Next**.

3. On the Select installation type page, click **Next**.

4. On the Select destination server page, click the **Server01** you want to install to and click **Next**.

5. On the Select server roles page, expand the **File and Storage Services** node, expand the **File and iSCSI Services** node, and then select the **File Server** role. Click **Next**.

6. On the Select features page, click **Next**.

7. On the Confirm installations selections page, click **Install**.

8. When the installation is complete, click **Close**.

9. Click **Manage > Add Roles and Features**.

10. When the Add Roles and Features Wizard opens, on the Before You Begin page, click **Next**.

11. On the Select installation type page, click **Next**.

12. On the Select destination server page, click the **Server02** you want to install to and then click **Next**.

13. On the Select server roles page, expand the File and Storage Services node, expand the File and iSCSI Services node, and select the File Server role. Click **Next**.

14. On the Select features page, click **Next**.

15. On the Confirm installations selections page, click **Install**.

16. When the installation is complete, click **Close**.

17. Using Server Manager, click **Tools > Failover Cluster Manager**.

18. In the left-hand pane, expand the cluster node, expand the **Storage** node and then click the **Pools** node, as shown in Figure 2-4.

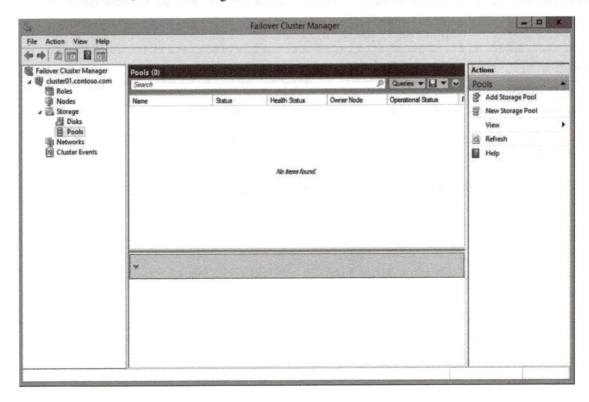

Figure 2-4
The Pools node

19. Right-click on **Pools** and choose **New Storage Pool**.

20. When the New Storage Pool Wizard opens, on the Before You Begin page, click **Next**.

21. On the Storage Pool Name page, in the Name text box, type **StoragePool**. Then select the second **Cluster1**. Click **Next**.

22. Select the three disks and then click **Next**.

23. On the Confirmation page, click **Create**.

24. When the storage pool is created, click **Close**.

25. Right-click the storage pool and choose **New Virtual Disk**.

26. When the New Virtual Disk Wizard opens, on the Before You Begin page, click **Next**.

27. On the Storage Pool page, click **StoragePool** and then click **Next**.

28. On the Virtual Disk Name page, In the Name text boxes, type **StorageDisk**. Click **Next**.

29. On the Storage Layout page, click **Simple**. Click **Next**.

30. On the Size page, specify **12 GB** and then click **Next**.

31. On the Confirmation page, click **Create**.

32. After the virtual disk is created, the create a volume when this wizard closes option is already selected. Click **Close**.

33. When the New Volume wizard opens, on the Before You Begin page, click **Next**.

34. On the Server and Disk page, verify the **12 GB** disk that needs to be provisioned and then click **Next**.

35. On the Size page, specify the size of the volume and then click **Next**.

36. On the Drive Letter or Folder page, select the desired drive letter, and then click **Next**.

37. On the File System Settings page, for the Volume label text box, type **Storage** and then click **Next**.

38. On the confirmation page, click **Create**.

39. When the volume is created, click **Close**.

40. Take a screen shot of Computer Management by pressing Alt+Prt Scr and then paste it into your Lab 2 worksheet file in the page provided by pressing Ctrl+V.

End of exercise. You can leave the Server Manager open for the next exercise.

Exercise 2.6	Implementing Cluster Aware Updating
Overview	In this exercise, you will install and enable cluster aware updating.
Mindset	Why is Cluster Aware Updating important to clusters?
Completion time	20 minutes

1. Log into Storage01 as **contoso\administrator** with the password of **Pa$$w0rd**.

2. On Storage01, using the Server Manager console, open the **Manage** menu and click Add Roles and Features.

3. When the Add Roles and Features Wizard starts, click **Next**.

4. On the Select installation type page, click **Next**.

5. On the Select destination server page, click **Next**.

6. On the Select server roles page, click **Next**.

7. On the Select features page, click to select the **Remote Server Administration Tools**. When it asks you to add features, click **Add Features**. Expand Remote Server Administration Tools, expand Feature Administration Tools, and expand Failover Cluster Tools.

8. Select **Failover Cluster Management Tools, Failover Cluster Module for Windows PowerShell, Failover Cluster Automation Server**, and **Failover Cluster Command Interface**. Click **Next**.

9. On the Web Server Role (IIS) page, click **Next**.

10. On the Select role services page, click **Next**.

11. On the Confirm installation selections page, click **Install**.

12. When the installation is complete, click **Close**.

13. On Storage01, using **Server Manager**, open the **Tools** menu and click **Cluster-Aware Updating**.

14. When the Cluster-Aware Updating dialog box opens (as shown in Figure 2-5), type **cluster1**, and click **Connect**.

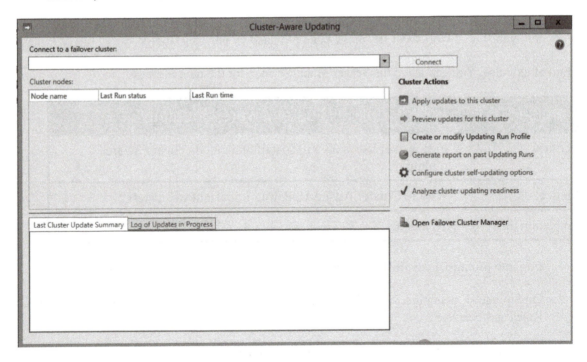

Figure 2-5
Specifying the cluster address

15. After a minute or so, click **Configure cluster self-updating options**.

16. When the Configure Self-Updating Options Wizard opens, click Next.

17. Select the **Add the CAU clustered role, with self-updating mode enabled, to this cluster**. click **Next**.

Question 4	By default, how often does it schedule updates for a cluster?

18. On the Specify self-updating schedule page, click **Next**.

19. On the Advanced Options page, click **Next**.

20. On Additional Update Options page, click **Next**.

21. On the Confirmation page, click **Apply**.

22. When the wizard is complete, click **Close**.

23. Close **Cluster-Aware Updating**.

End of exercise. Close any open windows before you begin the next exercise.

LAB REVIEW QUESTIONS

Completion time   10 minutes

1. In Exercise 2.1, what was used to connect to an iSCSI target?

2. In Exercise 2.2, how is failover clustering defined in Server Manager, a role or a feature?

3. In Exercise 2.3, before creating the failover cluster, what should you do first to make sure that your servers will support the failover clustering.

4. In Exercise 2.4, why was the 2 GB volume used when configuring the quorum?

5. In Exercise 2.5, what were the three high-level steps to create and use a clustered storage space?

6. In Exercise 2.6, what is used to install updates to nodes in a failover cluster?

7. In Exercise 2.6, in which group of features do you find the Cluster Aware Updating?

Lab Challenge	Upgrading a Failover Cluster
Overview	To complete this challenge, you will describe to perform upgrade a failover cluster writing the high-level steps of upgrading a failover cluster.
Mindset	You have a failover cluster running on Windows Server 2008 R2. You want to upgrade the cluster to Windows Server 2012 R2. What method would you use to upgrade the cluster to clean servers running Windows Server 2012 R2?
Completion time	10 minutes

End of lab. You can log off or start a different lab. If you want to restart this lab, you'll need to click the End Lab button in order for the lab to be reset.

LAB 3
MANAGING FAILOVER CLUSTERING

THIS LAB CONTAINS THE FOLLOWING EXERCISES AND ACTIVITIES:

Exercise 3.1   Deploying the General Use File Server Role

Exercise 3.2   Deploying a Scale-Out File Server

Exercise 3.3   Configuring Failover and Preference Settings

Exercise 3.4   Managing a Cluster and Cluster Nodes

Exercise 3.5   Destroying a Cluster

Lab Challenge   Configuring VM Monitoring

BEFORE YOU BEGIN

The lab environment consists of student workstations connected to a local area network, along with a server that functions as the domain controller for a domain called contoso.com. The computers required for this lab are listed in Table 3-1.

Table 3-1
Computers required for Lab 3

Computer	Operating System	Computer Name
Server (VM 1)	Windows Server 2012 R2	RWDC01
Server (VM 2)	Windows Server 2012 R2	Server01
Server (VM 3)	Windows Server 2012 R2	Server02
Server (VM 4)	Windows Server 2012 R2	Storage01

In addition to the computers, you will also require the software listed in Table 3-2 to complete Lab 3.

Table 3-2
Software required for Lab 3

Software	Location
Lab 3 student worksheet	Lab3_worksheet.docx (provided by instructor)

Working with Lab Worksheets

Each lab in this manual requires that you answer questions, shoot screen shots, and perform other activities that you will document in a worksheet named for the lab, such as Lab03_worksheet.docx. You will find these worksheets on the book companion site. It is recommended that you use a USB flash drive to store your worksheets, so you can submit them to your instructor for review. As you perform the exercises in each lab, open the appropriate worksheet file, fill in the required information, and save the file to your flash drive.

After completing this lab, you will be able to:

■ Deploy a General Use File Server role

■ Deploy a Scale-Out File Server

■ Configure failover and preferences settings

■ Manage a cluster and cluster nodes

■ Destroy a cluster

■ Configure VM monitoring

Estimated lab time: 85 minutes

Exercise 3.1	Deploying the General Use File Server Role
Overview	To demonstrate using a failover cluster in this exercise, create a General Use File Server using the cluster that was created in Lab2, along with a shared iSCSI drive.
Mindset	What are the advantages of a General Use File Server over a Scale-Out File Server?
Completion time	20 minutes

1. Log into Server01 as **contoso\administrator** with the password of **P@$$w0rd**. Server Manager opens.

2. On Server01, using **Server Manager**, click **Tools > Failover Cluster Manager**. The Failover Cluster Manager opens.

3. On the Failover Cluster Manager, expand **Cluster1.contoso.com** and then right-click **Roles** and choose **Configure Role**.

4. When the High Availability Wizard opens, click **Next**.

5. On the Select Role page (as shown in Figure 3-1), click **File Server** and then click **Next**.

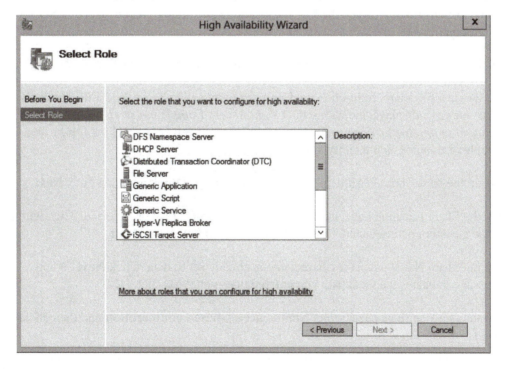

Figure 3-1
Selecting a role for the failover cluster

6. On the File Server Type page, click **File Server for general use** and then click **Next**.

7. On the Client Access Point page, type **FileServer** in the Name text box. Type **192.168.1.63** in the Address column and then click **Next**.

8. On the Select Storage page, click to select the **Cluster Disk 2** and then click **Next**.

9. On the Confirmation page, click **Next**.

10. On the Summary page, click **Finish**.

11. In the Failover Cluster Manager, click **Roles** (if it is not already selected or highlighted).

12. Take a screen shot of the Failover Cluster Manager by pressing Alt+Prt Scr and then paste it into your Lab 3 worksheet file in the page provided by pressing Ctrl+V.

13. Click **Cluster1.contoso.com**. If the Current Host Server is Server02, right-click **Cluster1.contoso.com** and choose **More Actions > Move Core Cluster Resources > Select Node**. When the Move Cluster Resources dialog box opens, click **Server01** and then click **OK**.

14. Click the **Roles** node. If the Owner node is Server02, right-click File Server and choose **Move > Select Node**. When the Move Clustered Role dialog box opens, click **Server01** and then click **OK**.

15. Wait two minutes to allow time for the DNS entry to be created for FileServer.

16. To create a file share, right-click the **File Server** role and choose **Add File Share**. If an error message displays, indicating the *Client Access Point is not ready to be used for share creation*, the DNS entry for FileServer has not been created. Click **OK**, wait a couple of minutes, and then try again.

17. When the New Share Wizard opens, click **SMB Share-Quick** and then click **Next**.

18. On the Share Location page, ensure the File Server cluster role is selected. Then with the Type a custom path selected, type **e:\data** in the text box. Click **Next**.

19. On the Share Name page, the Share name is already set to data. Click **Next**. When a message indicates the local path you entered does not exist, click **OK**.

20. On the Other settings page, select **Enable access-based enumeration** and then click **Next**.

Question 1	*What does access-based enumeration do?*

21. On the Permissions page, view the current permissions and then click **Next**.

22. On the Confirmation page, click **Create**.

23. When the installation is complete, click **Close**.

24. With the FileServer role selected, click the **Resources** tab at the bottom of the console.

25. Take a screen shot of the Failover Cluster Manager by pressing Alt+Prt Scr and then paste it into your Lab 3 worksheet file in the page provided by pressing Ctrl+V.

26. Click the **Shares** tab.

27. Take a screen shot of the Failover Cluster Manager by pressing Alt+Prt Scr and then paste it into your Lab 3 worksheet file in the page provided by pressing Ctrl+V.

End of exercise. Leave the Failover Cluster Manager open for the next exercise.

Exercise 3.2	Deploying a Scale-Out File Server
Overview	In this exercise, you will remove the General Use File Server and install a Scale-Out File Server.
Mindset	How does a Scale-Out File Server differ from a General Use File Server?
Completion time	20 minutes

1. On Server01, using Failover Cluster Manager, right-click the **FileServer** role and choose **Remove**. When you are prompted to confirm this action, click **Yes**.

2. Expand the **Storage** node and then click **Disks**. Right-click **Cluster Disk 2 (Available Storage)** and choose **Add to Cluster Shared Volumes**. Notice that it is now assigned to Cluster Shared Volume.

3. Right-click **Roles** and choose **Configure Role**.

4. When the High Availability Wizard opens, click **Next**.

5. On the Select Role page, click **File Server** and then click **Next**.

6. On the File Server Type page, click **Scale-Out File Server for application data** and then click **Next**.

7. On the Client Access Point page, type **FileServer** in the Name text box. Click **Next**.

8. On the Confirmation page, click **Next**.

9. On the Summary page, click **Finish**.

10. Wait two minutes so that DNS entries have time to be created.

11. Click the **Roles** node. If the Owner node is Server02, right-click **File Server** and choose **Move > Select Node**. When the Move Clustered Role dialog box opens, click **Server01** and then click **OK**.

12. Click **Roles**. Right-click the **FileServer** role and choose **Add File Share**. Click **OK**.

    If an error message displays, indicating the *Client Access Point is not ready to be used for share creation*, the DNS entry for FileServer has not be created. Wait a couple of minutes, and then try again.

13. When the New Share Wizard opens, click **SMB Share – Quick** and then click **Next**.

14. On the Share Location page, click the **FileServer** and note that **Select by volume**: C:\ClusterStorage\Volume1 is already selected. Click **Next**.

15. On the Share Name page, type **Data** in the Share name text box and then click **Next**.

16. On the Other Settings page, click to select **Enable access-based enumeration**, and then click **Next**.

17. On the Permissions page, click **Next**.

18. On the Confirm selections page, click **Create**.

19. When the installation is complete, click **Close**.

20. With the FileServer highlighted, click the **Shares** tab at the bottom of Failover Cluster Manager.

21. Take a screen shot of the Failover Cluster Manager by pressing Alt+Prt Scr and then paste it into your Lab 3 worksheet file in the page provided by pressing Ctrl+V.

End of exercise. Leave the Failover Cluster Manager open for the next exercise.

Exercise 3.3	Configuring Failover and Preference Settings
Overview	In this exercise, you will configure how the failover cluster will respond to failover and how it recovers from failover.
Mindset	
Completion time	10 minutes

1. On Server01, using Failover Cluster Manager, click **Roles**.

2. Right-click the **FileServer** role and choose **Properties**. The Properties dialog box opens, as shown in Figure 3-2.

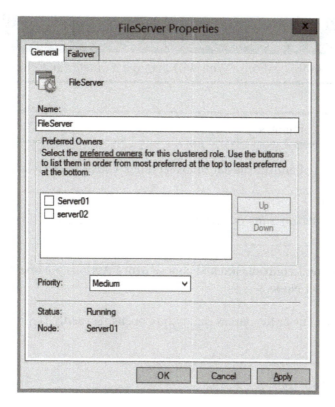

Figure 3-2
Configuring share settings

3. On the General tab, to make the Server01 the preferred owner, click to select **Server01**.

4. Click the **Failover** tab.

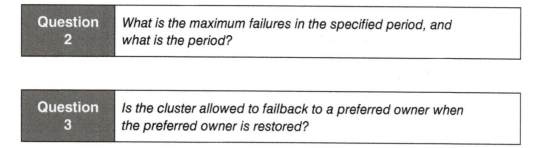

Question 2	*What is the maximum failures in the specified period, and what is the period?*

Question 3	*Is the cluster allowed to failback to a preferred owner when the preferred owner is restored?*

5. Click **OK** to close the Properties dialog box.

6. Right-click the **FileServer** role again and choose **Properties**.

7. On the General tab, uncheck **Server01** as the preferred owner.

8. Click **OK** to close the Properties dialog box.

End of exercise. Leave the Failover Cluster Manager open for the next exercise.

Exercise 3.4	Managing a Cluster and Cluster Nodes
Overview	In this exercise, you will manage a cluster and cluster nodes.
Mindset	
Completion time	15 minutes

1. On Server01, using Failover Cluster Manager, click **Cluster1.contoso.com**

Question 4	*Which is the current host server?*

2. Right-click **Cluster1.contoso.com** and choose **More Actions > Move Core Cluster Resources > Select Node**.

3. When the Move Cluster Resources dialog box opens, Server02 is already selected. Click **OK**.

Question 5	*Which is the current destination node?*

4. Click **Roles**.

Question 6	*Which is the owner for the FileServer role?*

5. Take a screen shot of the Failover Cluster Manager by pressing Alt+Prt Scr and then paste it into your Lab 3 worksheet file in the page provided by pressing Ctrl+V.

6. Right-click the **FileServer** role and choose **Move > Select Node**.

7. Click **Server02** and then click **OK**.

Question 7	*Which is the owner for the FileServer role?*

8. Reboot Server02.

9. Watch the **Failover Cluster Manager** on **Server01** and see how it responds. Wait until Server02 finishes rebooting.

Question 8	*Which is the owner for the FileServer role after Server02 comes back?*

10. To gracefully shut down Server01, right-click the **Server01** under the Nodes node and choose **Pause > Drain Roles**. Observe that Server02 replaces Server01 as the Owner Node.

11. Right-click **Server01** and choose **Resume > Fail Roles Back**. Observe that Server01 regains Owner Node status.

End of exercise. Leave the Failover Cluster Manager open for the next exercise.

Exercise 3.5	Destroying a Cluster
Overview	In this exercise, you will destroy a cluster.
Mindset	
Completion time	10 minutes

1. On Server01, using the Failover Cluster Manager, expand **Cluster1.contoso.com** and then click **Roles**.

2. Right-click the **FileServer** role and choose **Remove**. When you are prompted to confirm this action, click **Yes**.

3. Right-click **Cluster1.contoso.com** and choose **More Actions > Destroy Cluster**. When you are prompted to confirm that you want to permanently destroy the cluster, click **Yes**.

4. Close **Failover Cluster Manager**.

End of exercise. Close any open windows before you begin the next exercise.

LAB REVIEW QUESTIONS

Completion time 5 minutes

1. In Exercise 3.1, which console was used to create the File Server for the cluster?

2. In Exercise 3.3, how did you configure the preferred owner?

3. In Exercise 3.3, which tab was used to specify that fallback to occur only at night?

4. In Exercise 3.4, which option was clicked to drain the roles?

5. In Exercise 3.5, what had to be removed first before you could destroy the cluster?

Lab Challenge	Configuring VM Monitoring
Overview	To complete this challenge, you will describe how to configure monitoring of a failover cluster that is running within Hyper-V.
Mindset	You have created a failover using two VMs on a host running Hyper-V. How would you configure monitoring of the failover cluster?
Completion time	5 minutes

End of lab. You can log off or start a different lab. If you want to restart this lab, you'll need to click the End Lab button in order for the lab to be reset.

LAB 4
MANAGING VM MOVEMENT

THIS LAB CONTAINS THE FOLLOWING EXERCISES AND ACTIVITIES:

Exercise 4.1   Moving a VM Storage Location

Exercise 4.2   Moving a VM to Another Host

Exercise 4.3   Copying a VM

Exercise 4.4   Exporting and Importing a VM

Lab Challenge   Configuring Computers for Live Migration

BEFORE YOU BEGIN

The lab environment consists of student workstations connected to a local area network, along with a server that functions as the domain controller for a domain called contoso.com. The computers required for this lab are listed in Table 4-1.

Table 4-1
Computers required for Lab 4

Computer	Operating System	Computer Name
Server (VM 1)	Windows Server 2012 R2	RWDC01
Server (VM 2)	Windows Server 2012 R2	Server01
Server (VM 3)	Windows Server 2012 R2	Server02

In addition to the computers, you will also require the software listed in Table 4-2 to complete Lab 4.

Table 4-2
Software required for Lab 4

Software	Location
Lab 4 student worksheet	Lab4_worksheet.docx (provided by instructor)

Working with Lab Worksheets

Each lab in this manual requires that you answer questions, shoot screen shots, and perform other activities that you will document in a worksheet named for the lab, such as Lab04_worksheet.docx. You will find these worksheets on the book companion site. It is recommended that you use a USB flash drive to store your worksheets, so you can submit them to your instructor for review. As you perform the exercises in each lab, open the appropriate worksheet file, fill in the required information, and save the file to your flash drive.

After completing this lab, you will be able to:

- Move a virtual machine file to a different location

- Move a virtual machine to another host

- Make a copy of a virtual machine

- Export and import a virtual machine

- Configure computers for live migration

Estimated lab time: 65 minutes

Exercise 4.1	Moving a VM Storage Location
Overview	In this exercise, you will use the Hyper-V console to create a virtual machine, and move the storage location of a virtual machine to another storage location.
Mindset	Hyper-V supports three types of migration. What are the three types of migration and when would you use each one?
Completion time	20 minutes

1. Log into Server02 as **contoso\administrator** with the password of **Pa$$w0rd**. Server Manager opens.

2. On Server02, using **Server Manager**, click **Tools > Hyper-V Manager**. The Hyper-V Manager opens.

3. On Hyper-V Manager, right-click **Server02** and choose **New > Virtual Machine**.

4. When the New Virtual Machine Wizard starts, click **Next**.

5. On the Specify Name and Location, Type **TestVM**. Then click to select the Store the virtual machine in a different location. In the Location text box, type **C:\VM**, as shown in Figure 4-1. Click **Next**.

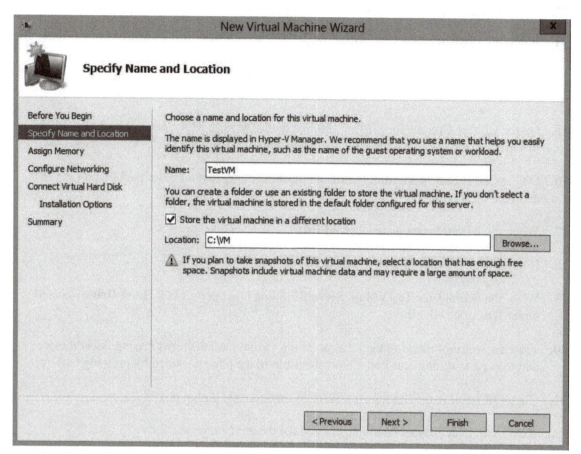

Figure 4-1
Selecting images to use

6. On the Specify Generation page, Generation 1 is already selected. Click **Next**.

7. On the Assign Memory page, specify **256** MB startup memory, click to select **Use Dynamic Memory for this virtual machine**. If a message displays, indicating *Out of Bounds* (caused by the amount of memory available), ignore the error. Click **Next**.

8. On the Configure Networking page, click **Next**.

9. On the Connect virtual hard disk page, type **TestVM.vhdx** in the Name: text box and then specify **5** GB for the size. Click **Next**.

10. On the Installation Options page, since this VM is to be used only for VM manipulation and not to actually run Windows (virtual machines cannot run on Hyper-V that is running on a virtual machine), leave the **Install an operating system later** option selected and click **Next**.

11. When the wizard is complete, click **Finish**.

12. In the Virtual machines section, click Server02, right-click **TestVM** and choose **Move**.

13. When the Move Wizard starts, click **Next**.

14. On the Choose Move Type page, click **Move the virtual machine's storage** and then click **Next**.

15. On the Choose Options for Moving Storage dialog wizard, Move all of the virtual machine's data to a single location is already selected. Click **Next**.

16. On the Choose a new location for virtual machine page, in the Folder page, type **C:\VM2** and then click **Next**.

17. When the wizard is complete, click **Finish**.

18. Right-click the **TestVM** and choose **Settings**.

19. When the Settings for TestVM on Server02 dialog box opens, click **Hard Drive** (located under IDE Controller 0).

20. Take a screenshot showing the location of the virtual hard disk by pressing Alt+Prt Scr and then paste it into your Lab 4 worksheet file in the page provided by pressing Ctrl+V.

21. Click **OK** to close the Settings for TestVM on Server02 dialog box.

End of exercise. Leave Hyper-V Manager open for the next exercise.

Exercise 4.2	Moving a VM to Another Host
Overview	In this exercise, you will use the storage migration to move a VM to a second Hyper-V host.
Mindset	
Completion time	15 minutes

1. On Server02, using Hyper-V Manager, right-click **Server02** and choose **Hyper-V Settings**.

2. When the Hyper-V Settings dialog box opens, in the server section, click **Live Migrations**.

3. In the Incoming live migrations, select **Use any available network for live migration**.

4. Click **OK** to close the Hyper-V Settings dialog box.

5. Log into Server01 as **contoso\administrator** with the password of **Pa$$w0rd**. Server Manager opens.

6. Using Server01, click **Tools > Hyper-V Manager**.

7. Using Hyper-V Manager, right-click **Server01** and choose **Hyper-V Settings**.

8. When the Hyper-V Settings dialog box opens, in the server section, click **Live Migrations**.

9. In the Incoming live migrations, select **Use any available network for live migration**.

10. Click **OK** to close the Hyper-V Settings dialog box.

11. On Server02, In the Virtual machines section, right-click **TestVM** and choose **Move**.

12. When the Move Wizard starts, click **Next**.

13. On the Choose Move Type page opens, the Move the virtual machine is already selected. Click **Next**.

14. On the Specify Destination Computer page, type **Server01** in the Name text box and then click **Next**.

Question 1	What is the most important thing that you have to check when moving a VM to another host?

15. On the Chose Move Options page, Move the virtual machine's data to a single location is already selected. Click **Next**.

16. On the Choose a new location for virtual machine, and type **C:\VM** in the Folder text box and then click **Next**.

17. When the wizard is complete, click **Finish**.

18. On Server01, using **Hyper-V Manager**, click **Server01**. TestVM should appear in the Virtual Machines section.

19. Take a screenshot of the Hyper-V Manager on Server01 by pressing Alt+Prt Screen and then paste it into your Lab 4 worksheet file in the page provided by pressing Ctrl+V.

End of exercise. Leave Hyper-V Manager open for the next exercise.

Exercise 4.3	Copying a VM
Overview	In this exercise, you will export and import a virtual machine using Hyper-V.
Mindset	You are working with another partner company, which created a virtual machine running Windows Server 2012 R2, which has several customized programs and services that you would like to implement at your company. Instead of going through the actual installation and configuration, you would like to implement a copy of the VM on your Hyper-V Host. What should you do?
Completion time	10 minutes

1. On Server01, using **Hyper-V Manager**, right-click **TestVM** and choose **Export**.

2. When the Export Virtual Machine dialog box opens, type **C:\BAK** and then click **Export**.

3. Right-click **Server01** and choose **Import Virtual Machine**.

4. When the Import Virtual Machine wizard starts, click **Next**.

5. On the Location Folder page, type **C:\Bak\TestVM** in the Folder text box and then click **Next**.

6. On the Select Virtual Machine page, the **TestVM** is already selected. Click **Next**.

7. On the Choose Import Type page, click **Copy the virtual machine (create a new unique ID)** and then click **Next**.

Question 2	*Which option is used to import a VM multiple times?*

8. On the Choose Folders for Virtual Machine Files page, click to select the **Store the virtual machine in a different location**. In the Virtual machine configuration folder text box, Snapshot store text box, and Smart Paging folder textbox, type **C:\VM2** and then click **Next**.

9. On the Choose Folders to Store Virtual Hard Disk page, type **C:\VM2** in the Location text box and then click **Next**.

10. On the Completing Import Wizard, click **Finish**.

11. Take a screenshot showing Hyper-V Manager with both virtual machines TestVM by pressing Alt+Prt Scr and then paste it into your Lab 4 worksheet file in the page provided by pressing Ctrl+V.

End of exercise. Close any open windows before you begin the next exercise.

LAB REVIEW QUESTIONS

Completion time	5 minutes

1. In Exercise 4.1, which migration option was used to move a VM from one drive to another drive?

2. In Exercise 4.3, which option was used to take an existing set of VM files and recreate the exact same VM?

3. In Exercise 4.3, which option was used when importing a virtual machine that just allows Hyper-V to bring in the virtual machine as-is?

Lab Challenge	Configuring Computers for Live Migration
Overview	To complete this challenge, you will explain how to configure computers for live migration by writing the necessary high-level steps.
Mindset	Two Hyper-V hosts are clustered together. How would you configure the source and destination computers for live migration?
Completion time	15 minutes

Write out the steps you performed to complete the challenge.

End of lab. You can log off or start a different lab. If you want to restart this lab, you'll need to click the End Lab button in order for the lab to be reset.

LAB 5
CONFIGURING ADVANCED FILE SOLUTIONS

THIS LAB CONTAINS THE FOLLOWING EXERCISES AND ACTIVITIES:

Exercise 5.1   Creating an NFS Shared Folder

Exercise 5.2   Installing and Configuring BranchCache

Exercise 5.3   Using File Classification

Exercise 5.4   Configuring File Access Auditing

Lab Challenge   Creating an NFS Shared Folder on a Cluster

BEFORE YOU BEGIN

The lab environment consists of student workstations connected to a local area network, along with a server that functions as the domain controller for a domain called contoso.com. The computers required for this lab are listed in Table 5-1.

Table 5-1

Computers required for Lab 5

Computer	Operating System	Computer Name
Server (VM 1)	Windows Server 2012 R2	RWDC01
Server (VM 2)	Windows Server 2012 R2	Server01
Server (VM 3)	Windows Server 2012 R2	Server02

In addition to the computers, you will also require the software listed in Table 5-2 to complete Lab 5.

Table 5-2

Software required for Lab 5

Software	Location
Lab 5 student worksheet	Lab05_worksheet.docx (provided by instructor)

Working with Lab Worksheets

Each lab in this manual requires that you answer questions, shoot screen shots, and perform other activities that you will document in a worksheet named for the lab, such as Lab05_worksheet.docx. You will find these worksheets on the book companion site. It is recommended that you use a USB flash drive to store your worksheets, so you can submit them to your instructor for review. As you perform the exercises in each lab, open the appropriate worksheet file, fill in the required information, and save the file to your flash drive.

After completing this lab, you will be able to:

- Create an NFS shared folder

- Install and configure BranchCache

- Configure file classification using FSRM

- Enable and configure file access auditing

- Create an NFS shared folder on a cluster

Estimated lab time: 110 minutes

Exercise 5.1	Creating an NFS Shared Folder
Overview	In this exercise, you will install the Sever for NFS role. You will then share a folder so that it can be used by NFS clients.
Mindset	How does NFS differ from SMB?
Completion time	20 minutes

1. Log into Server01 as **contoso\administrator** with the password of **Pa$$w0rd**.

2. When Server Manager opens, click **Manage** and then click **Add Roles and Features**. The Add Roles and Feature Wizard opens.

3. On the Before you begin page, click **Next**.

4. Select Role-based or feature-based installation and then click **Next**.

5. On the Select destination server page, click **Server01.contoso.com** and then click **Next**.

6. On the Select server roles page, expand **File and Storage Services**, expand **File and iSCSI Services**, and click to select **Server for NFS**. Click **Next**.

7. When you are prompted to add features required for Server for NFS, click **Add Features**. On the Select server roles page, click **Next**.

8. On the Select features page, click to select **Client for NFS** and then click **Next**.

9. On the Confirm installation selections page, click **Install**.

10. When the installation is complete, click **Close**.

11. On Server01, using Server Manager, click **Tools > Services for Network File System (NFS)**. The Services for Network File System console opens.

12. Right-click the **Services for NFS** node and choose **Properties**. The Services for NFS Properties dialog box opens.

13. Click to select **Active Directory domain name**. In the Active Directory domain name text box, type **contoso.com**.

14. Click **OK** to close the Services for NFS Properties dialog box.

15. Open the File Explorer by clicking the **File Explorer** icon on the taskbar.

16. Click the Local Disk (C:) and create the **C:\Data** folder.

17. Right-click **C:\Data** and choose **Properties**. The Properties dialog box opens.

18. Click the **NFS Sharing** tab.

19. Click **Manage NFS Sharing**. The NFS Advanced Sharing dialog box appears as shown in Figure 5-1.

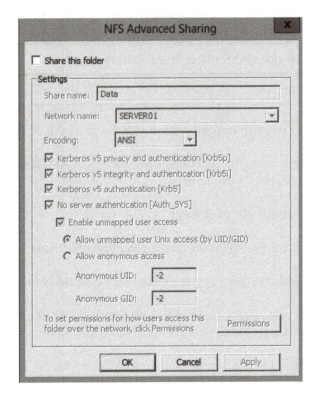

Figure 5-1
Sharing a folder for NFS

20. Select the **Share this folder** check box.

21. In the NFS Advanced Sharing dialog box, click **Permissions**. The NFS Share Permissions dialog box appears.

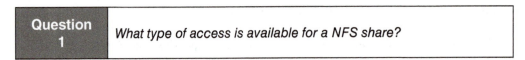

Question 1	*What type of access is available for a NFS share?*

22. Click **OK** to close the NFS Share Permissions dialog box.

23. Click **OK** to close the NFS Advanced Sharing dialog box.

24. Click **Close** to close the Data Properties dialog box.

25. Close **File Explorer**.

26. Close Services for Network File System.

End of exercise. Close any open windows before you begin the next exercise.

Exercise 5.2	Installing and Configuring BranchCache
Overview	In this exercise, you will install and configure BranchCache so that it can be used with websites and file shares.
Mindset	What do you need to use to enable a website to be cached by BranchCache and what do you need to enable a shared folder to be cached by BranchCache?
Completion time	30 minutes

1. On Server01, using Server Manager, click **Manage** and then click **Add Roles and Features**. The Add Roles and Feature Wizard opens.

2. When the Add Roles and Features Wizard opens, click **Next**.

3. On the Select Installation Type page, make sure that **Role-based or feature-based installation** is selected and then click **Next**.

4. On the Select destination server page, click **Server01.contoso.com** and then click **Next**.

5. In Select Server Roles, under Roles, expand **File and Storage Services** and then expand **File and iSCSI Services**. Click to select the check box for **BranchCache for Network Files**. Click **Next**.

6. In Select features, click **BranchCache** and then click **Next**.

7. On the Confirm installation selections page, click **Install**. When installation is complete, click **Close**.

8. Login into RWDC01 as **contoso\administrator** with the password of **Pa$$w0rd**.

9. On RWDC01, when Server Manager opens, click **Tools > Active Directory Users and Computers**.

10. When the Active Directory Users and Computers console open, right-click **contoso.com** and choose **New > Organizational Unit**.

11. When the New Object – Organization Unit dialog box opens, type **Servers** in the Name text box. Click **OK**.

12. Close **Active Directory Users and Computers**.

13. On RWDC01, using Server Manager, click **Tools > Group Policy Management**. The Group Policy Management console opens.

14. Navigate to and right-click the **Servers** OU and choose **Create a GPO in this domain, and Link it here**.

15. When the New GPO dialog box opens, type **BranchCache for Servers** in the Name text box.

16. Click **OK** to close the New GPO dialog box.

17. Expand the **Servers** OU and then right-click the **BranchCache for Servers** GPO and choose **Edit**.

18. When the Group Policy Management Editor opens, expand the following path: **Computer Configuration, Policies, Administrative Templates, Network**. Under **Network**, click **Lanman Server**.

| Question 2 | *What must all servers in a BranchCache infrastructure have?* |

19. Double-click **Hash Publication for BranchCache**. The Hash Publication for BranchCache dialog box opens as shown in Figure 5-2.

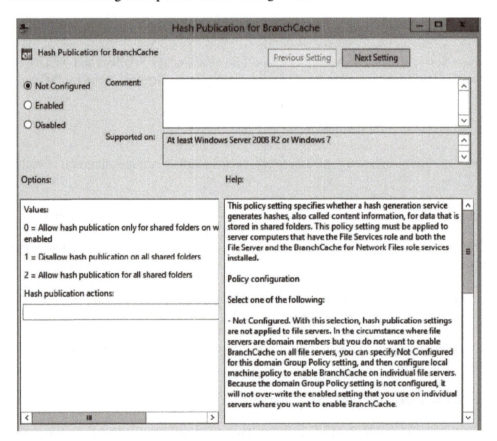

Figure 5-2
Enabling hash publication for BranchCache

20. In the Hash Publication for BranchCache dialog box, click **Enabled**.

21. In Options, **Allow hash publication for all shared folders** is already selected. To enable hash publication for all shared folders in all file servers that you add to the OU, click **Allow hash publication for all shared folders**.

22. Click **OK** to close the Hash Publication for BranchCache dialog box.

23. Close **Group Policy Management Editor**.

24. On Server01, open File Explorer by clicking the **File Explorer** icon on the task bar.

25. Create a folder named **C:\SharedFolder**.

26. Right-click the **C:\SharedFolder** and choose **Properties**.

27. Click the **Sharing** tab.

28. Click **Advanced Sharing**.

29. Click **Share this folder** and then click **OK** to close the Advanced Sharing dialog box.

30. Click **Close** to close the SharedFolder Properties dialog box.

31. Close **File Explorer**.

32. On Server01, using **Server Manager**, click **Tools > Computer Management**.

33. When the Computer Management console opens, under **System Tools**, expand **Shared Folders** and then click **Shares**.

34. In the details pane, right-click **SharedFolder** and choose **Properties**. The share's Properties dialog box opens.

35. In the Properties dialog box, on the General tab, click **Offline Settings**. The Offline Settings dialog box opens.

36. Ensure that **Only the files and programs that users specify are available offline** is selected and then click **Enable BranchCache**.

37. Click **OK** twice.

38. Close **Computer Management**.

39. On RWDC01, using Group Policy Management, expand **Group Policy Objects**, and then right-click **Default Domain Policy** and choose **Edit**.

Question 3	*By default, which BranchCache cache mode is used by Windows 8 machines?*

40. When the Group Policy Management Editor opens, navigate to the **Computer Configuration > Policies > Administrative Templates > Network** node and click **BranchCache**.

41. Double-click **Set BranchCache Distributed Cache mode**.

42. When the **Set BranchCache Distributed Cache mode** dialog box opens, click **Enabled**.

43. Click **OK** to close the Set BranchCache Distributed Cache mode.

44. Close **Group Policy Management Editor**.

45. Close **Group Policy Management**.

End of exercise. Close any open windows before you begin the next exercise.

Exercise 5.3	Using File Classification
Overview	In this exercise, you will use File Server Resource Manager to classify files in a folder.
Mindset	What are the two components needed to classify a file?
Completion time	25 minutes

1. On Server01, open File Explorer by clicking the **File Explorer** icon on the Taskbar.

2. Navigate to and open the **C:\SharedFolder**.

3. Right-click the empty white space of the **C:\SharedFolder** and choose **New > Rich Text Document**.

4. Name the document **Doc1** and press **Enter**.

5. Close **Windows Explorer**.

6. On Server01, using **Server Manager**, click **Manage** and then click **Add Roles and Features**.

7. When the Add Roles and Feature Wizard opens, click **Next**.

8. Select Role-based or feature-based installation and then click **Next**.

9. Click **Select a server from the server pool**, click **Server01.contoso.com**, and then click **Next**.

10. Scroll down and expand **File and Storage Services** and expand **File and iSCSI Services**. Select **File Server Resource Manager**.

11. When you are prompted to add features, click **Add Features**.

12. On the Select server roles page, click **Next**.

13. On the Select features page, click **Next**.

14. On the Confirm installation selections, click **Install**.

15. When the installation is complete, click **Close**.

16. On Server01, using **Server Manager**, click **Tools > File Server Resource Manager**.

17. When the File Server Resource Manager opens, expand **Classification Management**. When you are done, the File Resource Manager should look like Figure 5-3.

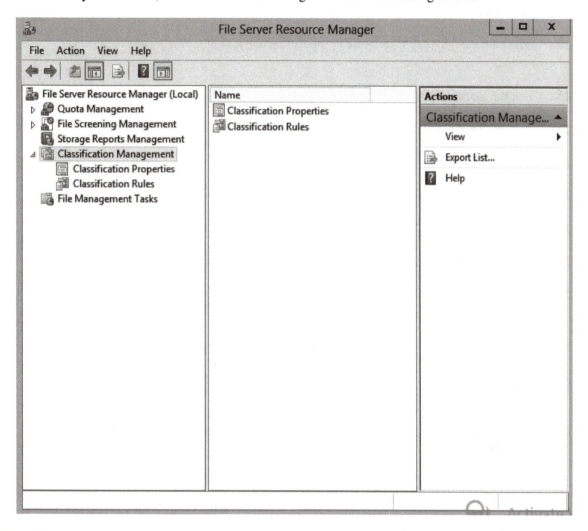

Figure 5-3
Opening the File Server Resource Manager

18. Click **Classification Properties**.

19. Right-click **Classification Properties** and choose **Create Local Property**. The Create Local Classification Property dialog box opens.

20. In the **General** tab, Type **FileClass** in the Name text box.

21. For the Property type, select **Yes/No** and then click **OK**.

22. Click **Classification Rules**.

23. Right-click **Classification Rules** and choose **Create Classification Rule**. The Create Classification Rule dialog box opens.

24. In the General tab, type **ClassRule** in the Rule name text box. Make sure the rule is enabled.

25. Click the **Scope** tab.

26. Click the **Add** button. Navigate to the **C:\SharedFolder** and then click **OK**.

27. Click the **Classification** tab.

28. In the Classification method section, select **Folder Classifier**.

29. Under Property, **FileClass**, and **Yes** should already be selected in the Property section.

30. Click the **Evaluation Type** tab.

31. Click to select the **Re-evaluate existing property values**. Aggregate the values should already be selected.

32. Click **OK** to close the Create Classification Rule dialog box.

33. In File Server Resource Manager, under Actions, click **Run Classification with All Rules Now**.

34. When the Run Classification dialog box opens, click **Wait for classification to complete**. Click OK.

35. If a Windows Internet Explorer 10 dialog box appears, click **Don't use recommended settings** and then click **OK**.

36. When the classification is complete, the Automatic Classification Report opens. You should see one file is classified.

37. Take a screenshot showing the Automatic Classification Report by pressing Alt+Prt Scr and then paste it into your Lab 5 worksheet file in the page provided by pressing Ctrl+V.

38. Close the **Automatic Classification Report**.

39. Close **File Server Resource Manager**.

End of exercise. Close any open windows before you begin the next exercise.

Exercise 5.4	Configuring File Access Auditing
Overview	In this exercise, you will use a group policy to enable file object auditing. You will then enable auditing in a folder.
Mindset	What are the components that must be configured to enable auditing of a folder or file?
Completion time	20 minutes

1. On RWDC01, using **Server Manager**, click **Tools > Group Policy Management**.

2. When the Group Policy Management console opens, expand the **Domain Controllers** to show the Default Domain Controllers Policy. Then right-click **the Default Domain Controllers Default Policy** and choose **Edit**.

3. When the Group Policy Management Editor appears, expand **Computer Configuration, Policies, Windows Settings, Security Settings, Advanced Audit Policy Configuration, Audit Policies**, and then click **Audit Policies** (as shown in Figure 5-4).

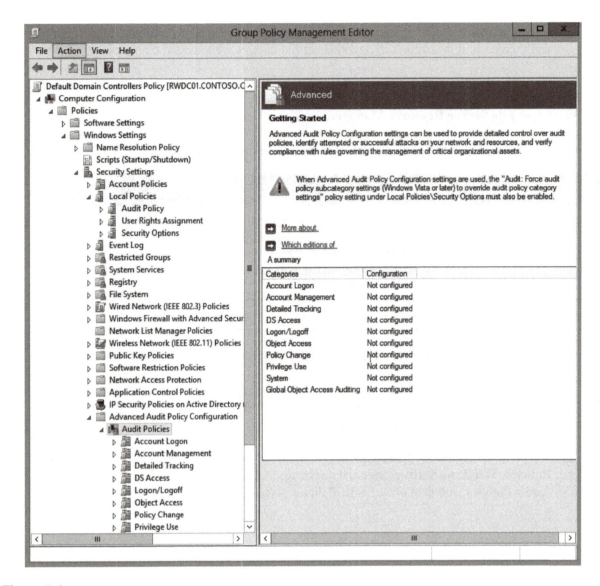

Figure 5-4
Configuring an audit policy

Question 4	Which audit policies are defined by default?

4. In the left pane, click **Object Access** and then double-click **Audit File System**. The Audit File Share Properties dialog box opens.

5. On the Audit File System Properties dialog box, click to select **Configure the following audit events** and then click to select **Success** and **Failure**.

6. Click **OK** to close the Audit File System Properties dialog box.

7. Close the **Group Policy Management Editor**.

8. Close **Group Policy Management**.

9. On Server01, open the File Explorer by clicking the **File Explorer** icon on the taskbar.

10. Navigate to and right-click **C:\SharedFolder** folder, choose **Properties**, and then click the **Security** tab.

11. Click the **Advanced** button. The Advanced Security Settings for SharedFolder dialog box opens.

12. In the Advanced Security Settings for Updates dialog box, click the **Auditing** tab, as shown in Figure 5-5.

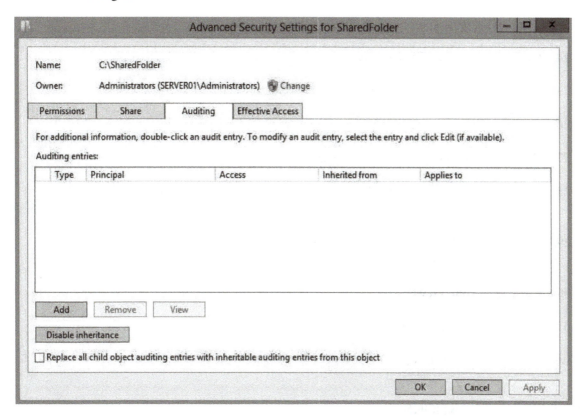

Figure 5-5
Enabling auditing for a folder

13. To add an auditing entry, click **Add**. The Auditing Entry for Data dialog box opens.

14. To specify a user or group, click **Select a principal**.

15. When the Select User, Computer, Service Account, or Group dialog box opens, type **domain users** in the text box and then click **OK**.

16. For Type, select **All**.

17. For the Permissions, click **Full Control**.

18. Click **OK** to close the Auditing Entry for SharedFolder dialog box.

19. On the Advanced Security Settings for SharedFolder dialog box, select to enable **Replace all child object auditing entries with inheritable auditing entries from this object**.

20. Click **OK** to close the Advanced Security Settings for SharedFolder dialog box.

21. Click **OK** to close the SharedFolder Properties dialog box.

22. Open a command prompt and execute the following command:

    ```
    gpupdate /force
    ```

23. Close the command prompt.

24. On Server01, using **File Explorer**, navigate to and open the **C:\SharedFolder** folder.

25. Right-click **Doc1** and choose **Delete**.

26. On Server01, using **Server Manager**, click **Tools > Event Viewer**.

27. Expand **Windows logs** and then click **Security**.

28. Look for entries that indicate that someone tried to delete a file or actions that involve the Recycle Bin.

29. Take a screen shot of the Event Viewer by pressing Alt+Prt Scr and then paste it into your Lab 5 worksheet file in the page provided by pressing Ctrl+V.

30. Close the **Event Viewer**.

31. Close **Windows Explorer**.

End of exercise. Close any open windows before you begin the next exercise.

LAB REVIEW QUESTIONS

Completion time   10 minutes

1. In Exercise 5.1, what is used to enable NFS sharing for AIX and Linux users?

2. In Exercise 5.2, how do you enable a hosted cache mode on a server running Windows Server 2012 R2?

3. In Exercise 5.2, what is the path to the hash publication policy in a GPO?

4. In Exercise 5.3, what do you need to do after you change or create classification properties or classification rule?

5. In Exercise 5.4, which type of audit policy was used to enable auditing of only files and folders?

Lab Challenge	Creating an NFS Shared Folder on a Cluster
Overview	To complete this challenge, you will describe how to create an NFS Shared folder on a cluster.
Mindset	What would be the general steps be to implement highly available NFS data store?
Completion time	5 minutes

End of lab. You can log off or start a different lab. If you want to restart this lab, you'll need to click the End Lab button in order for the lab to be reset.

LAB 6
IMPLEMENTING DYNAMIC ACCESS CONTROL

THIS LAB CONTAINS THE FOLLOWING EXERCISES AND ACTIVITIES:

Exercise 6.1   Using Dynamic Access Control (DAC)

Exercise 6.2   Implementing a Central Access Policy

Lab Challenge   Performing Access-Denied Remediation

BEFORE YOU BEGIN

The lab environment consists of student workstations connected to a local area network, along with a server that functions as the domain controller for a domain called contoso.com. The computers required for this lab are listed in Table 6-1.

Table 6-1
Computers required for Lab 6

Computer	*Operating System*	*Computer Name*
Server (VM 1)	Windows Server 2012 R2	RWDC01
Server (VM 2)	Windows Server 2012 R2	Server01

In addition to the computers, you will also require the software listed in Table 6-2 to complete Lab 6.

Table 6-2
Software required for Lab 6

Software	Location
Lab 6 student worksheet	Lab06_worksheet.docx (provided by instructor)

Working with Lab Worksheets

Each lab in this manual requires that you answer questions, shoot screen shots, and perform other activities that you will document in a worksheet named for the lab, such as Lab06_worksheet.docx. You will find these worksheets on the book companion site. It is recommended that you use a USB flash drive to store your worksheets, so you can submit them to your instructor for review. As you perform the exercises in each lab, open the appropriate worksheet file, fill in the required information, and save the file to your flash drive.

After completing this lab, you will be able to:

- Enable and configure DAC

- Create and implement a Central Access Policy

- Enable Access-Denied Assistant

Estimated lab time: 90 minutes

Exercise 6.1	Using Dynamic Access Control (DAC)
Overview	In this exercise, you will configure Dynamic Access Control by enabling KDC support for claims and creating a resource property and resource rule.
Mindset	How does Dynamic Access Control allow you to secure files for an organization?
Completion time	40 minutes

1. Log in to RWDC01 as **contoso\administrator** with the password of **Pa$$w0rd**.

2. In Server Manager, click **Tools > Group Policy Management**.

3. In the Group Policy Management console, expand **contoso.com** and then expand **Domain Controllers**. Then right-click Default Domain Controllers Policy and choose Edit.

4. In the Group Policy Management Editor, navigate to **Computer Configuration\Policies\Administrative Templates\System\KDC** and double-click **KDC support for claims, compound authentication, and Kerberos Armoring**.

5. Click **Enabled**. Under Options, Supported is already selected.

6. Take a screen shot of the KDC support for claims, compound authentication and Kerberos Armoring dialog box by pressing Alt+Prt Scr and then paste it into your Lab 6 worksheet file in the page provided by pressing Ctrl+V.

7. Click **OK** to close the KDC support for claims, compound authentication, and Kerberos armoring dialog box.

8. Close **Group Policy Management Editor**.

9. Close **Group Policy Management**.

10. On RWDC01, using **Server Manager**, click **Tools > Active Directory Administrative Center**. The Active Directory Administrative Center opens.

11. Navigate to the **Dynamic Access Control** node and then click the **Claim Types** container, as shown in Figure 6-1.

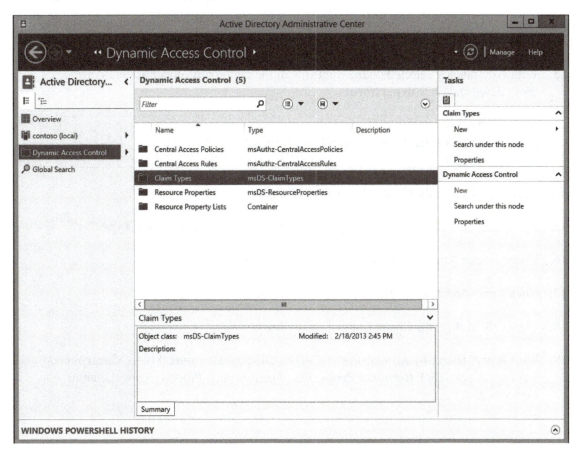

Figure 6-1
Opening Dynamic Access Control

12. In the Tasks pane, under Claim Types, click **New** and then click **Claim Type**. The Create Claim Type dialog box opens (see Figure 6-2).

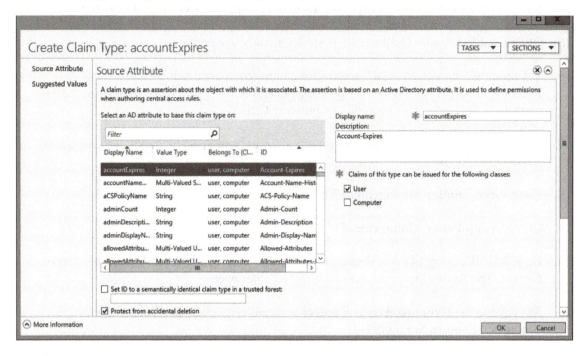

Figure 6-2
Creating a claim type

13. With User already selected on the right side of the dialog box, under Source Attribute, scroll down and click **department**.

Question 1	*What is the default display name?*

14. Click **OK** to close the Create Claim Type dialog box.

15. In the Tasks pane, under Claim Types, click **New** and then click **Claim Type**.

16. Under Source Attribute, scroll down and click **description**.

17. Click to deselect **User** and click to select **Computer**.

18. Click **OK** to close the Create Claim Type dialog box.

19. With Active Directory Administrative Center, click the **Dynamic Access Control** node and then double-click **Resource Properties**. The Resource Properties are shown in Figure 6-3.

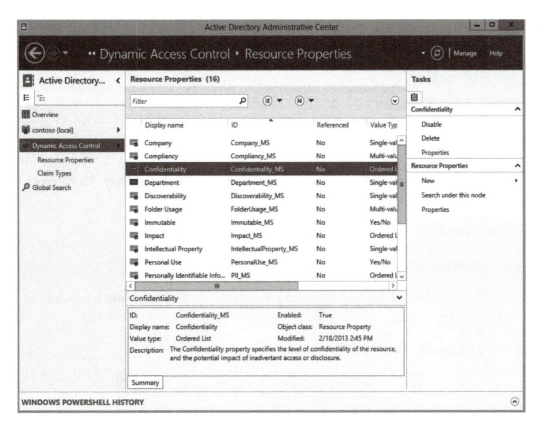

Figure 6-3
Viewing resource properties

20. To enable the Department resource property, under Resource Properties, right-click **Department** and choose **Enable**.

21. To enable the Confidentiality resource property, under Resource Property, right-click **Confidentiality** and choose **Enable**. Close Resource Properties.

22. Close **Active Directory Administrative Center**.

23. Log into Server01 as **contoso\administrator** with the password of **Pa$$w0rd**.

24. Open the **File Explorer** icon on the **Taskbar**.

25. Navigate to and open the **C:\SharedFolder**.

26. Right-click the empty white space of the **SharedFolder** window and choose **New > Rich Text Document**.

27. For the name of the document, type **Doc1** and then press **Enter**.

28. On Server01, using **Server Manager**, click **Tools > File Server Resource Manager**.

29. In File Server Resource Manager, expand **Classification Management** and then click **Classification Properties**.

30. Right-click **Classification Properties** and choose **Refresh**. The Confidentiality and Department appear with a Global scope.

Question 2	*What are the two classifications properties that have a global scope?*

31. Click **Classification Rules**.

32. Right-click **Classification Rules** and choose **Create Classification Rule**. The Create Classification Rule dialog box opens.

33. In the General tab, in the Rule name text box, type **Confidentiality**.

34. Click the **Scope** tab.

35. At the bottom of the dialog box, click **Add**. Browse to the **C:\SharedFolder** folder and then click **OK**.

36. Click the **Classification** tab (see Figure 6-4).

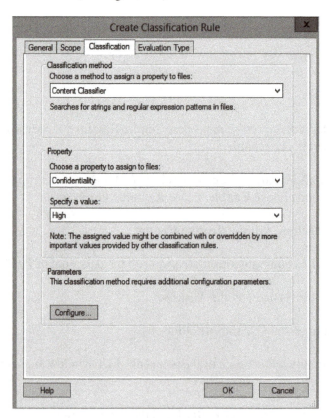

Figure 6-4
Creating a classification rule

37. The Classification method should already be set at Content Classifier and Property should be set at Confidentiality and High. To configure the Classification parameter, under Parameters, click **Configure**. The Classification Parameters dialog box opens.

38. Change the Regular expression to **String**. Under Expression, type **HR**, as shown in Figure 6-5. This means that if any document contains the string **HR**, that document will be automatically tagged as High confidentiality.

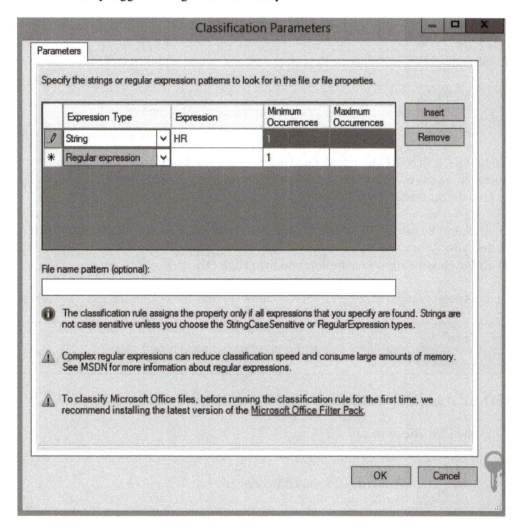

Figure 6-5
Defining a classification parameter

39. Click **OK** to close the Classification Parameters dialog box.

40. Click **Evaluation Type** tab.

41. Click to select **Re-evaluate existing property values**. Then select **Overwrite the existing value**.

42. Click **OK** to close the Create Classification Rule dialog box.

43. In File Server Resource Manager, under the Actions pane, click **Run Classification with All Rules Now**. When you are prompted to choose how you want to run the classification rules, click **Wait for classification to complete**.

44. Take a screen shot of File Server Resource Manager showing the Run Classification dialog box by pressing Alt+Prt Scr and then paste it into your Lab 6 worksheet file in the page provided by pressing Ctrl+V.

45. Click **OK**.

46. In the Automatic Classification Report, review the results and then close the report.

Question 3	How many files and properties does the report show?

47. Go to the **C:\SharedFolder** folder and double-click the **Doc1** document. When the document opens in WordPad, type **HR** and then close WordPad. When you are prompted to save the document, click **Save**.

48. Go back to **File Server Resource Manager** and then click **Run Classification with All Rules Now**. When you are prompted to select how to run the classification rules, click **Wait for classification to complete** and then click **OK**.

49. In the Automatic Classification Report window, review the results and close the report.

Question 4	How many files and properties does the report show?

50. Go back to the **C:\SharedFolder** folder. Right click **Doc1** and choose **Properties**.

51. Click the **Classification** tab.

Question 5	What is the Confidentiality set to?

52. Take a screen shot of File Server Resource Manager by pressing Alt+Prt Scr and then paste it into your Lab 6 worksheet file in the page provided by pressing Ctrl+V.

53. Click **OK** to close the Properties dialog box.

54. Close **File Server Resource Manager**. Close all other open windows.

End of exercise. Close any open windows before you begin the next exercise.

Exercise 6.2	Implementing a Central Access Policy
Overview	In this exercise, you will create and deploy a Central Access Policy, which is eventually applied using group policies.
Completion time	30 minutes

1. On Server01, click the **File Explorer** icon on the Taskbar.

2. Right-click the **C:\SharedFolder** folder and choose **Properties**. The Properties dialog box opens.

3. Click the **Security** tab.

4. Click the **Advanced** button. The Advanced Security Settings dialog box opens.

5. Click **Add**. The Permission Entry for SharedFolder dialog box opens.

6. Click **Select a principal**. In the Select User, Computer, Service Account, or Group dialog box, type **domain users** and then click **OK**.

Question 6	*What are the default basic permissions?*

7. At the bottom of the dialog box, click **Add a condition**.

8. For the condition, configure the following:

    Resource > Confidentiality > Equals > Value > High

    When you are done, the condition should look like Figure 6-6. Click **OK**.

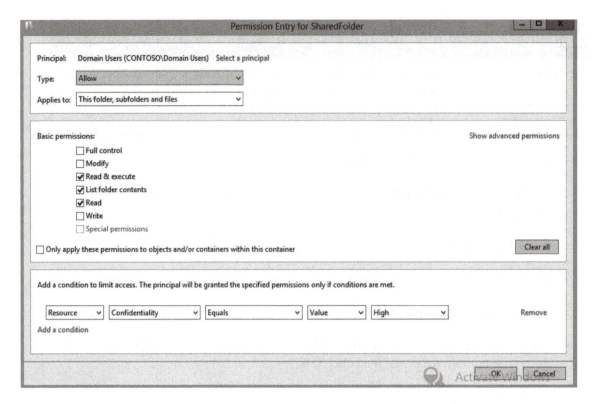

Figure 6-6
Define permissions based on a resource

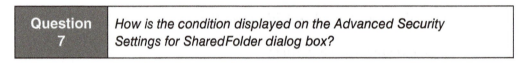

Question 7	How is the condition displayed on the Advanced Security Settings for SharedFolder dialog box?

9. Click **OK** to close the Advanced Security Settings for SharedFolder dialog box.

10. Click **OK** to close the Properties dialog box.

11. On RWDC01, using Server Manager, click **Tools > Active Directory Administrative Center**.

12. On RWDC01, in the Active Directory Administrative Center, navigate to and click the **Dynamic Access Control** node.

13. Double-click **Central Access Policies**. The Central Access Policies opens as shown in Figure 6-7.

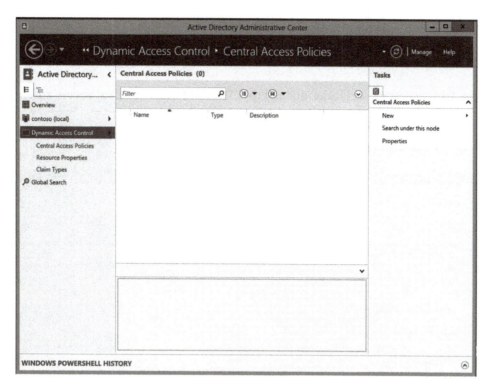

Figure 6-7
Viewing Central Access Policies.

14. Under Tasks, click **New > Central Access Policy**. The Central Access Policy dialog box opens as shown in Figure 6-8.

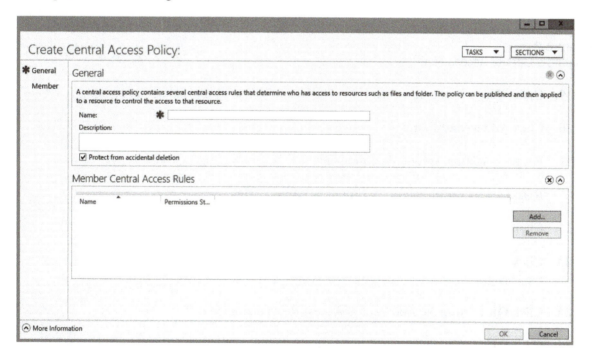

Figure 6-8
Creating a Central Access Policy

15. In the name text box, type **CentralAccessPolicy1**.

16. In the Member Central Access Rules section, click **Add**.

17. In the Add Central Access Rules dialog box, click **Add a new central access rule**.

18. In the Create Central Access Rules dialog box (as shown in Figure 6-9), in the Name text box, type **CentralAccessRule1**.

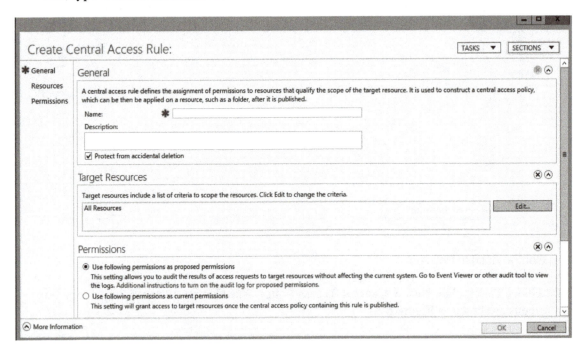

Figure 6-9
Creating a Central Access Rule

19. Under Target Resources, click **Edit**. The Central Access Rule dialog box opens.

20. Click **Add a condition**.

21. For the condition, specify the following:

    Resource > Confidentiality > Equals > Value > High

22. Click **OK** to close the Central Access Rule dialog box.

23. Click **OK** to close the Create Central Access Rule dialog box. Click **Yes** to save the changes.

24. Click **OK** to close the Add Central Access Rules dialog box.

25. Click **OK** to close the Create Central Access Policy dialog box.

26. Close the Active Directory Administrative Center.

27. On RWDC01, using **Server Manager**, click **Tools > Group Policy Management**.

28. In the Group Policy Management console, right-click the **Default Domain Policy** and choose **Edit**.

29. Navigate to **Computer Configuration\Policies\Windows Settings\Security Settings** and expand **File System**.

30. Right-click **Central Access Policy** and choose **Manage Central Access Policies**.

31. In the Central Access Policies Configuration dialog box (Figure 6-10), click **CentralAccessPolicy1** and then click **Add**. Click **OK**.

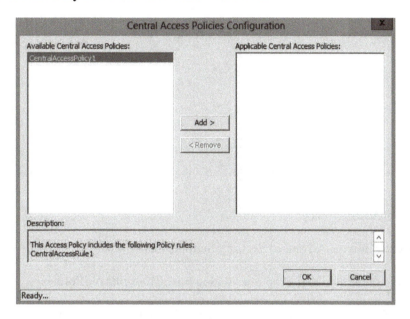

Figure 6-10
Deploying a Central Access Policy

32. On Server01, right-click the **Start** menu and choose **Command Prompt (Admin)**.

33. At the command prompt, execute the gpupdate /force command.

34. Close the Command Prompt.

34. Click the **File Explorer** icon on the Taskbar.

35. Navigate to **C:\SharedFolder**.

36. Right-click **Doc1** and choose **Properties**.

38. Click the **Security** tab and then click the **Advanced** button.

39. Click the **Central Policy** tab.

40. On the Central Policy tab (as shown in Figure 6-11), select **CentralAccessPolicy1** in the drop-down box and then click Change.

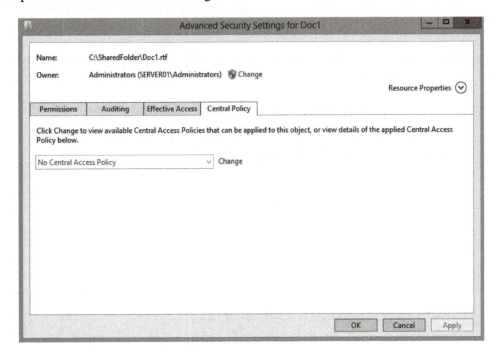

Figure 6-11
Configuring a Central Access Policy

41. Click **OK** to close the Advanced Security Settings dialog box.

42. Click **OK** to close the Doc1 Properties dialog box. Close **SharedFolder**.

End of exercise. Close any open windows before you begin the next exercise.

LAB REVIEW QUESTIONS

Completion time	10 minutes

1. In Exercise 6.1, how is KDC enabled to support for claims?

2. In Exercise 6.1, what tool is used to create and manage Dynamic Access Control?

3. In Exercise 6.1, to use Dynamic Access Control, what two components are created?

4. In Exercise 6.1, which Windows component is used in order to see how the classification rules were applied to a folder?

5. In Exercise 6.2, which program was used to create a Central Access Policy?

6. In Exercise 6.2, what is used to apply the Central Access Policy?

Lab Challenge	Performing Access Denied Remediation
Overview	To complete this challenge, you will describe how to enable access-denied remediation by writing the steps for the following scenario.
Mindset	You have just established a Central Access Policy that identifies human resource documents and assigns certain permissions to the documents. What steps are used to enable Access–Denied Assistance so that when a user is denied access to a message, a customized message is displayed for the user to call the help desk for further assistance?
Completion time	10 minutes

Write out the steps you performed to complete the challenge.

End of lab. You can log off or start a different lab. If you want to restart this lab, you'll need to click the End Lab button in order for the lab to be reset.

LAB 7
CONFIGURING AND OPTIMIZING STORAGE

THIS LAB CONTAINS THE FOLLOWING EXERCISES AND ACTIVITIES:

Exercise 7.1   Removing an iSCSI Target

Exercise 7.2   Creating and Configuring an iSCSI Target

Exercise 7.3   Configuring iSCSI Initiator

Exercise 7.4   Configuring Tiered Storage

Exercise 7.5   Using Features on Demand

Lab Challenge   Implementing Thin Provisioning

BEFORE YOU BEGIN

The lab environment consists of student workstations connected to a local area network, along with a server that functions as the domain controller for a domain called contoso.com. The computers required for this lab are listed in Table 7-1.

Table 7-1

Computers required for Lab 7

Computer	Operating System	Computer Name
Server (VM 1)	Windows Server 2012 R2	RWDC01
Server (VM 2)	Windows Server 2012 R2	Server01
Server (VM 3)	Windows Server 2012 R2	Server02
Server (VM 4)	Windows Server 2012 R2	Storage01

In addition to the computers, you will also require the software listed in Table 7-2 to complete Lab 7.

Table 7-2

Software required for Lab 7

Software	Location
Lab 7 student worksheet	Lab07_worksheet.docx (provided by instructor)

Working with Lab Worksheets

Each lab in this manual requires that you answer questions, shoot screen shots, and perform other activities that you will document in a worksheet named for the lab, such as Lab07_worksheet.docx. You will find these worksheets on the book companion site. It is recommended that you use a USB flash drive to store your worksheets, so you can submit them to your instructor for review. As you perform the exercises in each lab, open the appropriate worksheet file, fill in the required information, and save the file to your flash drive.

After completing this lab, you will be able to:

■ Remove, create, and configure an iSCSI Target

■ Configure an iSCSI Initiator

■ Use Features on Demand

■ Configure tiered storage

■ Implement thin provisioning

Estimated lab time: 125 minutes

Exercise 7.1	Removing an iSCSI Target
Overview	There is already an iSCSI Target on Storage01. In this exercise, you will remove the iSCSI target from Storage01 so that it can be recreated in the following exercises.
Completion time	25 minutes

1. Log in to Storage01 as **contoso\administrator** with the password of **Pa$$w0rd**.

2. In Server Manager , click **File and Storage Services** and then click **iSCSI**, as shown in Figure 7-1.

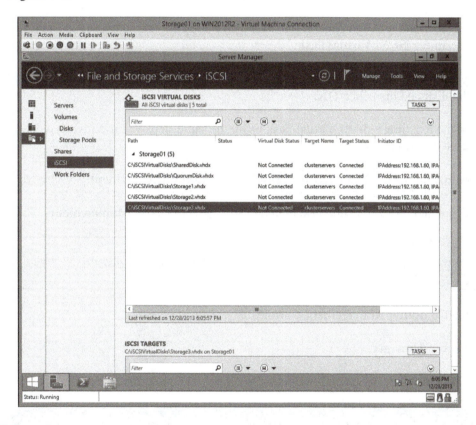

Figure 7-1

ISCSI devices shown in Server Manager

3. Right-click each iSCSI virtual disk and choose **Disable iSCSI Virtual Disk**. When you are prompted to confirm, click **Yes**.

4. Log in to Server01 as **contoso\administrator** with the password of **Pa$$w0rd**.

5. On Server01, in Server Manager, click **Tools > iSCSI Initiator**.

6. In the iSCSI Initiator Properties dialog box, click the **Volumes and Devices** tab.

7. Click the **Clear** button to remove all devices.

8. Click the **Discovery** tab.

9. In the Target portals section, click **Storage01** and then click **Remove**.

10. Click **OK** to close the iSCSI Imitator Properties dialog box.

11. Log in to Server02 as **contoso\administrator** with the password of **Pa$$w0rd**.

12. In Server Manager, click **Tools > iSCSI Initiator**.

13. Similar to what you did with Server01, disconnect the iSCSI target on Server02.

14. Click **OK** to close the iSCSI Imitator Properties dialog box.

15. On Storage01, on the iSCSI page, right-click the first iSCSI virtual drive listed and choose **Remove iSCSI Virtual Disk**.

16. When you are prompted to confirm, click to select the **Delete the iSCSI virtual disk file from the disk** and then click **OK**.

17. Remove the remaining iSCSI Virtual Disk using the same steps you used when deleting the first iSCSI virtual disk.

18. On Server01, in Server Manager, click **Tools > Computer Management**.

19. In the Computer Management console, under **Storage**, click **Disk Management**.

Question 1	*How many disks are displayed and what are the disks?*

20. Close the **Computer Management** console.

21. Close **Server Manager**.

End of exercise. Close any open windows before you begin the next exercise.

Exercise 7.2	Creating and Configuring an iSCSI Target
Overview	In this exercise, you will create and configure two iSCSI targets.
Mindset	To support an iSCSI Target, what roles must be installed?
Completion time	20 minutes

1. On Storage01, open **Server Manager**. Click **File and Storage Services** and then click **iSCSI**.

2. On the iSCSI page (as shown in Figure 7-2), click the **To create an iSCSI virtual disk, start the New iSCSI Virtual Disk Wizard** link.

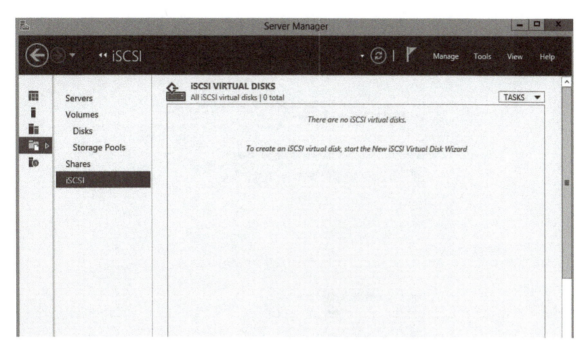

Figure 7-2
Viewing the iSCSI virtual disks section

3. On the Select iSCSI Virtual Disk Name page, Select by volume is already selected. Answer the following question and then click **Next**.

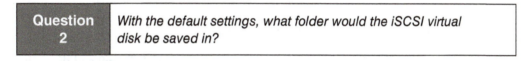

Question 2	*With the default settings, what folder would the iSCSI virtual disk be saved in?*

4. For the iSCSI Virtual Disk Location, type **QuorumDrive** in the Name text box and then click **Next**.

5. On the Specify iSCSI virtual disk size page, specify **2** GB and then click **Next**.

6. On the Assign iSCSI target page, click **New iSCSI target**. Click **Next**.

7. On the Target Name and Access page, type **ClusterGroup1** in the Name text box and then click **Next**.

8. On the Specify access servers page, click **Add** to open the Add imitator ID dialog box (see Figure 7-3).

Figure 7-3
Adding an initiator ID

9. Click to select **Enter a value for the selected type**.

10. For the Type, select **IP address**. In the Value text box, type **192.168.1.60** and then click **OK**.

11. Click **Add** again to open another Add initiator ID dialog box.

12. Click to select **Enter a value for the selected type**.

13. For the Type, select **IP address**. In the Value text box, type **192.168.1.70** and then click **OK**.

14. Back on the Specify access servers page, click **Next**.

15. On the Enable Authentication page, click **Next**.

16. On the Confirmation page, click **Create**.

17. When the iSCSI virtual disk is created, click **Close**.

18. On the iSCSI page, click **Tasks > New iSCSI Virtual Disk**.

19. On the Select iSCSI virtual disk location page, Select by volume is already selected. Click **Next**.

20. For the iSCSI Virtual Disk Name, type **DataDrive** in the Name text box and then click **Next**.

21. On the Specify iSCSI virtual disk size, specify **8 GB** and then click **Next**.

22. On the Assign iSCSI target page, Existing iSCSI target and clustergroup1 are already selected. Click **Next**.

23. On the Confirmation page, click **Create**.

24. When the iSCSI virtual disk is created, click **Close**.

Question 3	What is the status of the virtual disks?

25. Take a screen shot of the iSCSI page by pressing Alt+Prt Scr and then paste it into your Lab 7 worksheet file in the page provided by pressing Ctrl+V.

End of exercise. Leave Server Manager open.

Exercise 7.3	Configuring iSCSI Initiator
Overview	In this exercise, you will configure a server to connect to the iSCSI target that you created in Exercise 7.2 and then you will prepare the drive for usage.
Completion time	25 minutes

1. On Server01, using the Server Manager console, click **Tools > iSCSI Initiator**.

2. In the iSCSI Initiator properties dialog box, click the **Discovery** tab.

3. On the Discovery tab (as shown in Figure 7-4), click the **Discover Portal** button.

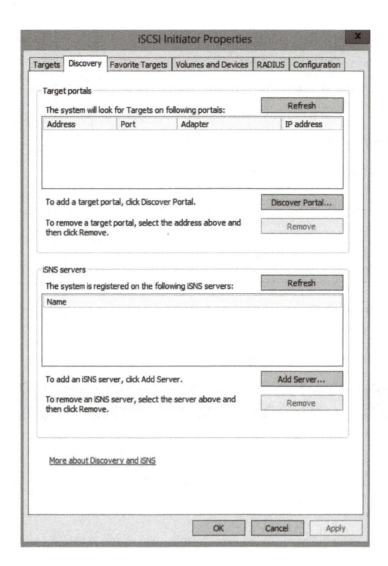

Figure 7-4
Discovering iSCSI targets

4. In the Discover Target Portal dialog box, type **192.168.1.80** in the IP address or DNS name text box.

Question 4	What is the default port for iSCSI?

5. Click **OK** to close the Discover Target Portal.

6. In the iSCSI Initiator Properties dialog box, click the **Targets** tab, click the Inactive discovered target, and then click the **Connect** button.

7. In the Connect To Target dialog box, click **OK**.

8. In the iSCSI Initiator Properties dialog box, click the **Volumes and Devices** tab.

9. Click the **Auto Configure** button.

Question 5	How many volumes are displayed

10. Take a screen shot of the Volumes and Devices tab window by pressing Alt+Prt Scr and then paste it into your Lab 7 worksheet file in the page provided by pressing Ctrl+V.

11. Click **OK** to close the iSCSI Initiator Properties dialog box.

12. On Server01, using Server Manager, click **Tools > Computer Management**.

13. Under Storage, click **Disk Management**.

Question 6	How many disks are displayed now?

14. Right-click Disk **1** and choose **Online**. Right-click Disk 1 and choose Initialize Disk. In the Initialize Disk dialog box, click **OK**.

Question 7	What partition style was used?

Question 8	What type of disk is Disk 1?

15. Right-click the 2.00 GB unallocated volume and choose **New Simple Volume**.

16. In the Welcome to the New Simple Volume Wizard, click **Next**.

17. On the Specify Volume Size, click **Next**.

18. On the Assign Drive Letter or Path page, click **Next**.

19. On the Format Partition page, in the Volume label text box, type **Quorum Drive**. Click **Next**.

20. When the wizard is complete, click **Finish**.

21. Using the previous steps, initialize, partition, and format Disk 2. Set the Volume label to **DataDrive**.

22. Take a screen shot of the Computer Management console showing the newly created disks by pressing Alt+Prt Scr and then paste it into your Lab 7 worksheet file in the page provided by pressing Ctrl+V.

23. Close **Computer Management**.

24. If you see any dialog boxes to format a drive, click Cancel.

25. Close **Server Manager.**

End of exercise. Close any open windows before you begin the next exercise.

Exercise 7.4	Configuring Tiered Storage
Overview	In this exercise, you will create a virtual disk using three SCSI disks. Since these disks are standard disk and not a combination of standard disks and SSD disks, you will be only creating a standard storage pool.
Completion time	20 minutes

1. On Storage01, open **Server Manager**.

2. Click **File and Storage Services**. Under **Volumes**, click **Disks** to view the current disks that are available.

3. Under Volumes, click **Storage Pools**.

4. In the main pane, under Storage Spaces, right-click **Primordial pool** and choose **New Storage Pool**.

5. On the Before you Begin page, click **Next**.

6. On the Storage Pool Name page, in the Name text box, type **TieredStorage**. Click **Next**.

7. On the Physical Disks page, select the three disks and then click **Next**.

8. On the Confirmation page, click **Create**.

9. When the Storage Pool is created, click **Close**.

10. Right-click the TieredStorage storage pool and choose **New Virtual Disk**.

11. In the New Virtual Disk Wizard, on the Before you Begin page, click **Next**.

12. On the Storage Pool page, select the storage pool that you just created and then click **Next**.

13. On the Virtual Disk Name page, in the Name text box, type **TieredDisk**.

Question 9	*Why can you not select the Create storage tiers on this virtual disk option?*

14. Click **Next**.

15. Click to select the Create storage tiers on the virtual disk. Click **Next**.

16. On the Storage layout page, click **Simple** and then click **Next**.

17. On the Provisioning page, Fixed provisioning type is already selected. Click **Next**.

18. Normally, you would be prompted to specify the maximum size for the faster tier (SSD) and the standard Tier (HDD). Instead, on the Size page, specify **12 GB** and then click **Next**.

19. On the Confirmation page, click **Create**.

20. When the virtual disk is created, click **Close**.

21. In the New Volume Wizard , on the Before You Begin page, click **Next**.

22. On the Server and Disk page, select **Storage01** and the associated disk. Click **Next**.

23. On the Size disk, specify **12 GB** and then click **Next**.

24. On the Drive Letter or Folder page, specify the desired drive letter and then click **Next**.

25. On the Select file system settings page, for the File system, select **NTFS**. In the Volume label text box, type **TieredStorage** and then click **Next**.

26. On the Confirmation page, click **Create**.

27. When the volume is created, click **Close**.

28. Take a screen shot of Server Manager by pressing Alt+Prt Scr and then paste it into your Lab 7 worksheet file in the page provided by pressing Ctrl+V.

End of exercise. You can close Server Manager open for the next exercise.

Exercise 7.5	Using Features on Demand
Overview	In this exercise, you will use Features on Demand to reduce the amount of disk space used by Windows.
Mindset	
Completion time	10 minutes

1. On Server01, open Windows PowerShell by clicking the **Windows PowerShell** icon on the task bar.

2. On Server01, execute the following command at the PowerShell prompt:

```
Get-WindowsFeature
```

3. Scroll up and find BitLocker Drive Encryption.

Question 10	*What is the status of BitLocker Drive Encryption?*

4. Take a screen shot of the Windows PowerShell window by pressing Alt+Prt Scr and then paste it into your Lab 7 worksheet file in the page provided by pressing Ctrl+V.

5. To remove the BitLocker binaries, execute the following command at the PowerShell prompt:

```
uninstall-WindowsFeature Bitlocker -Remove
```

6. Take a screen shot of the Windows PowerShell window by pressing Alt+Prt Scr and then paste it into your Lab 7 worksheet file in the page provided by pressing Ctrl+V.

7. Execute the following command at the PS prompt

```
Get-WindowsFeature
```

Question 11	*What is the status of BitLocker Drive Encryption?*

8. Close the Windows PowerShell window.

End of exercise. Close any open windows before you begin the next exercise.

LAB REVIEW QUESTIONS

Completion time   10 minutes

1. In Exercise 7.1, what task is necessary before you deleted the iSCSI targets?

2. In Exercise 7.2, what tool is used to manage the iSCSI targets?

3. In Exercise 7.2, what are the different ways to identify which clients can connect to an iSCSI target?

4. In Exercise 7.3, what port is used to connect to the iSCSI Target?

5. In Exercise 7.4, what are the two types of disks that make up tiered storage?

6. In Exercise 7.5, what Windows PowerShell command is used to view the Windows features that are available on a computer running Windows Server 2012 R2.

7. In Exercise 7.5, what Windows PowerShell cmdlet is used to remove the binaries of a Windows feature?

Lab Challenge	Implementing Thin Provisioning
Overview	To complete this challenge, you will describe how to implement thin provisioning by writing the steps for the following scenario.
Mindset	You are an administrator for the Contoso Corporation. You have several Hyper-V hosts that connect to a central Storage Area Network (SAN). You are close to running out of disk space on a couple of LUNS. What are the steps that you would perform to switch a disk that is thick provisioned to a disk that is thin provisioned?
Completion time	10 minutes

Write out the steps you performed to complete the challenge.

End of lab. You can log off or start a different lab. If you want to restart this lab, you'll need to click the End Lab button in order for the lab to be reset.

LAB 8
CONFIGURING AND MANAGING BACKUPS

THIS LAB CONTAINS THE FOLLOWING EXERCISES AND ACTIVITIES:

Exercise 8.1   Installing Windows Server Backup

Exercise 8.2   Performing a Manual Backup of a Local Volume to a Remote Share

Exercise 8.3   Backing up the System State

Exercise 8.4   Managing VSS Settings

Exercise 8.5   Enabling Shadow Copies for Shared Volumes

Lab Challenge   Using Hyper-V Snapshots

BEFORE YOU BEGIN

The lab environment consists of student workstations connected to a local area network, along with a server that functions as the domain controller for a domain called contoso.com. The computers required for this lab are listed in Table 8-1.

Table 8-1
Computers required for Lab 8

Computer	Operating System	Computer Name
Server (VM 1)	Windows Server 2012 R2	RWDC01
Server (VM 2)	Windows Server 2012 R2	Server01
Server (VM 3)	Windows Server 2012 R2	Server02
Server (VM 4)	Windows Server 2012 R2	Storage01

In addition to the computers, you will also require the software listed in Table 8-2 to complete Lab 8.

Table 8-2
Software required for Lab 8

Software	Location
Lab 8 student worksheet	Lab08_worksheet.docx (provided by instructor)

Working with Lab Worksheets

Each lab in this manual requires that you answer questions, shoot screen shots, and perform other activities that you will document in a worksheet named for the lab, such as Lab08_worksheet.docx. You will find these worksheets on the book companion site. It is recommended that you use a USB flash drive to store your worksheets, so you can submit them to your instructor for review. As you perform the exercises in each lab, open the appropriate worksheet file, fill in the required information, and save the file to your flash drive.

After completing this lab, you will be able to:

■ Install Windows Server Backup

■ Perform a manual backup of a local volume to a remote share

■ Back up files and the system state using Windows Server Backup

■ Manage VSS settings using VSSAdmin

■ Enable shadow copies for shared volumes

■ Use Hyper-V snapshots

Estimated lab time: 90 minutes

Exercise 8.1	Installing Windows Server Backup
Overview	In this exercise, you will install the Windows Server Backup feature, which will be used in the following exercises.
Mindset	What is the best method for data recovery?
Completion time	10 minutes

1. Log into Server02 as **contoso\administrator** with the password of **Pa$$w0rd**.

2. In Server Manager, click **Manage > Add Roles and Features**.

3. In the Add Roles and Features Wizard, click **Next**.

4. On the Select installation type page, click **Next**.

5. On the Select destination server page, click **Server02.contoso.com** and then click **Next**.

6. On the Select server roles screen, click **Next**.

7. Select **Windows Server Backup** and then click **Next**.

8. On the Confirm installation selections page, click **Install**.

9. When the installation is complete, click **Close**.

End of exercise. Leave Server Manager open.

Exercise 8.2	Performing a Manual Backup of Local Folders to a Remote Share
Overview	In this exercise, you will back up a data folder using Windows Server Backup
Mindset	How often should you backup a data folder that contains user data files?
Completion time	15 minutes

1. Log into Storage01 as **contoso\administrator** with the password of **Pa$$w0rd**.

2. Open the **File Explorer** icon on the task bar.

3. Navigate to Local Disk (C:) and create a **C:\BAK** folder.

4. Right-click the **BAK** folder and choose **Properties**.

5. In the Properties dialog box, click the **Sharing** tab.

6. Click the **Advanced Sharing** button.

7. In the Advanced Sharing dialog box, click to select the **Share this folder** option.

8. Click the **Permissions** button.

9. In the Permissions dialog box, with Everyone already selected, click the **Allow Change** box.

10. Click **OK** to close the Permissions dialog box.

11. Click **OK** to close the Advanced Sharing dialog box.

12. Click **Close** to close the BAK Properties dialog box.

13. In File Explorer, create folders named **C:\BAK\BAK1** and **C:\BAK\BAK2**.

14. On Server02, using Server Manager, click **Tools > Windows Server Backup**.

15. In the wbadmin window, click **Local Backup** (see Figure 8-1).

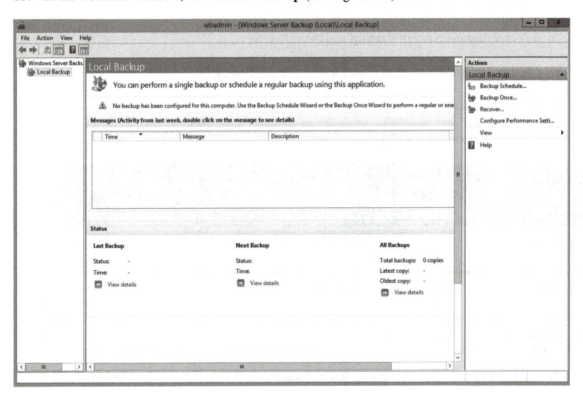

Figure 8-1
Opening Windows Server Backup

16. In the Actions panel, click **Backup Once**.

17. When prompted to select a Backup option, click **Different Options** and then click **Next**.

18. For the backup configuration, click **Custom** and then click **Next**.

19. On the Select Items for Backup page, click **Add Items** and then expand the **C** drive. Click to select the **Users** folder and the **ProgramData** folder (as shown in Figure 8-2) and then click OK.

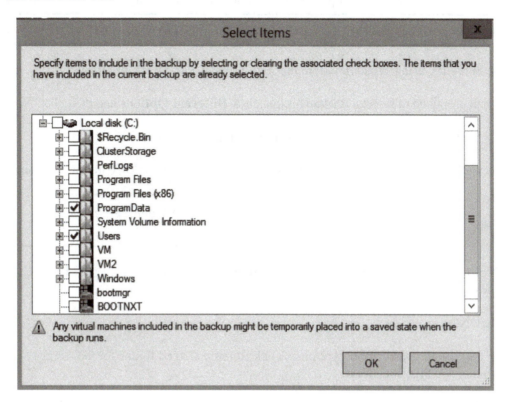

Figure 8-2
Selecting items to back up

Question 1	*What is the ProgramData folder used for?*

20. Click **Next** to continue.

21. On the Specify Destination Type page, click the **Remote shared folder** and then click **Next**.

22. On the Specify Remote Folder dialog box, type the location **\\storage01\BAK\BAK1** and then click **Next**.

23. On the Confirmation page, click **Backup**.

24. When the backup is complete, take a screen shot of wbadmin window by pressing Alt+Prt Scr and then paste it into your Lab 8 worksheet file in the page provided by pressing Ctrl+V.

25. Click **Close**.

End of exercise. Leave Wbadmin open for the next exercise.

Exercise 8.3	Backing Up the System State
Overview	In this exercise, you will back up the system state of a server.
Mindset	Why is it important to back up the system state?
Completion time	20 minutes

1. On Server02, using Wbadmin, from the Actions pane, click **Backup Once**.

2. When prompted to select a Backup option, click **Different Options** and then click **Next**.

3. For the backup configuration, click **Custom** and then click **Next**.

4. On the Select Items dialog box, click **Add** Items and then select **Bare metal recovery**.

Question 2	Which items were selected when you selected Bare metal recovery?

5. Click to deselect **Bare metal recovery**, **System Reserved drive**, and **Local Disk (C:)**. Click **OK**.

6. Click **Next**.

7. On the Specify Destination Type page, click **Remote shared folder** for the storage location and then click **Next**.

8. On the Specify Remote Folder dialog box, type the location **\\storage01\BAK\BAK2** and then click **Next**.

9. Confirm the settings and then click **Backup**.

10. When the backup is complete, take a screen shot of the Backup Once Wizard by pressing Alt+Prt Scr and then paste it into your Lab 8 worksheet file in the page provided by pressing Ctrl+V.

11. Click Close.

12. Close Wbadmin.

End of exercise. Close any open windows before you begin the next exercise.

Exercise 8.4	Managing VSS Settings
Overview	In this exercise, you will use VSSAdmin to manage VSS, including identifying VSS writer and VSS provider.
Mindset	What advantage does VSS provide when you are performing backups?
Completion time	10 minutes

1. On Server02, right-click the **Start menu** and choose **Command Prompt (Admin)**.

2. In the Administrator: Command Prompt dialog box, execute the following command to see a list of commands supported with vssadmin:

```
vssadmin /?
```

3. Execute the following command to see a list of VSS writers on Server02 and their current state:

```
vssadmin list writers
```

Question 3	How many VSS writers do you have?

4. Execute the following command to see a list of VSS providers on Server02:

```
vssadmin list providers
```

Question 4	What are the VSS providers?

5. Execute the following command to see a list of existing volume shadow copies:

```
vssadmin list shadows
```

Question 5	How many shadows did you have?

6. To list the volumes that are eligible for shadow copies, execute the following command:

```
vssadmin list volumes
```

7. To view used, allocated, and maximum shadow copy storage space, execute the following command:

```
vssadmin list shadowstorage
```

8. Take a screen shot of the Command Prompt window by pressing Alt+Prt Scr and then paste it into your Lab 8 worksheet file in the page provided by pressing Ctrl+V.

9. Close the Administrator: Command Prompt window.

End of exercise. Close any open windows before you begin the next exercise.

Exercise 8.5	Enabling Shadow Copies for Shared Volumes
Overview	In this exercise, you will enable and configure shadow copies to automatically back up shared folders.
Mindset	What does Shadow Copies allow you to do?
Completion time	15 minutes

1. Log into Server01 as **contoso\administrator** with the password of **Pa$$w0rd**.

2. Using **File Explorer**, create a folder named **C:\CorpDocs**.

3. Share the **C:\CorpDocs** folder. Configure it so that **Everyone** has **Allow Change** share permission.

4. Open the **C:\CorpDocs** folder.

5. Create a text file in the CorpDocs folder named **Agenda.txt**, type your name in the **Agenda.txt** file, and then save and close the text file.

6. On Server01, using Server Manager, click **Tools > Computer Management**.

7. In Computer Management, expand the **Storage** node and then click **Disk Management**.

8. Right-click **C** drive and choose **Properties**.

9. Select the **Shadow Copies** tab.

10. Click to select the **C:** drive (as shown in Figure 8-3) and then click **Enable**.

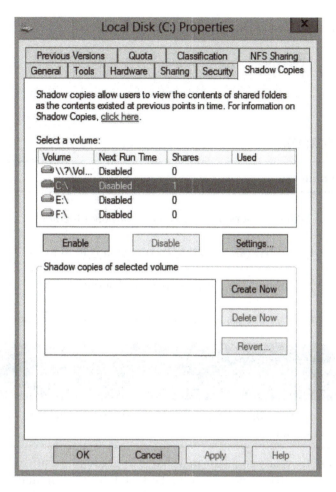

Figure 8-3
Configuring shadow copies

11. In the Enable Shadow Copies dialog box, click **Yes** to confirm you want to enable shadow copies on the volume.

12. Take a screen shot of the Properties window by pressing Alt+Prt Scr and then paste it into your Lab 8 worksheet file in the page provided by pressing Ctrl+V.

13. Click **Create Now** to create a second snapshot of the selected volume.

14. Click **Settings**.

15. In the Settings dialog box, click **Schedule**.

Question 6	How often are shadow copies created and at what time?

16. Click **OK** to close the C:\ dialog box.

17. Click **OK** to close the Settings dialog box.

18. Click **OK** to close the Local Disk (C:) Properties dialog box.

19. Close Computer Management.

End of exercise. Close any open windows before you begin the next exercise.

LAB REVIEW QUESTIONS

Completion time	10 minutes

1. In Exercise 8.1, is Windows Server Backup a role or is it a feature?

2. In Exercise 8.3, which Windows PowerShell command is used to list VSS writers?

3. In Exercise 8.3, which command is used to list the shadow copies?

4. In Exercise 8.4, where are the shadow copies enabled for a shared folder?

Lab Challenge	Using Hyper-V Snapshots
Overview	To complete this challenge, you will describe how to create Hyper-V snapshots.
Mindset	You are ready to perform a major upgrade to a critical application on Server01. You need to make sure that you can undo the changes if the upgrade does not go well. What should you do?
Completion time	10 minutes

Write out the steps you performed to complete the challenge.

End of lab. You can log off or start a different lab. If you want to restart this lab, you'll need to click the End Lab button in order for the lab to be reset.

LAB 9
RECOVERING SERVERS

THIS LAB CONTAINS THE FOLLOWING EXERCISES AND ACTIVITIES:

Exercise 9.1   Restoring a folder using Windows Server Backup

Exercise 9.2   Restoring the System State of a System

Exercise 9.3   Restoring a File Using Shadow Copy

Exercise 9.4   Booting Into Safe Mode

Exercise 9.5   Using Command Prompt Repair Tools

Lab Challenge   Performing an Authoritative Restore

BEFORE YOU BEGIN

The lab environment consists of student workstations connected to a local area network, along with a server that functions as the domain controller for a domain called contoso.com. The computers required for this lab are listed in Table 9-1.

Table 9-1
Computers required for Lab 9

Computer	Operating System	Computer Name
Server (VM 1)	Windows Server 2012 R2	RWDC01
Server (VM 2)	Windows Server 2012 R2	Server01
Server (VM 3)	Windows Server 2012 R2	Server02
Server (VM 4)	Windows Server 2012 R2	Storage01

In addition to the computers, you will also require the software listed in Table 9-2 to complete Lab 9.

Table 9-2
Software required for Lab 9

Software	Location
Lab 9 student worksheet	Lab09_worksheet.docx (provided by instructor)

Working with Lab Worksheets

Each lab in this manual requires that you answer questions, shoot screen shots, and perform other activities that you will document in a worksheet named for the lab, such as Lab09_worksheet.docx. You will find these worksheets on the book companion site. It is recommended that you use a USB flash drive to store your worksheets, so you can submit them to your instructor for review. As you perform the exercises in each lab, open the appropriate worksheet file, fill in the required information, and save the file to your flash drive.

After completing this lab, you will be able to:

■ Restore items using Windows Server Backup

■ Restore files using shadow copy

■ Boot the server into Safe mode

■ Boot the server into the command prompt and use basic troubleshooting tools to fix boot problems

Estimated lab time: 90 minutes

Exercise 9.1	Restoring a Folder Using Windows Server Backup
Overview	In this exercise, you will pick up where you left off in the last exercise by restoring a folder that you backed up.
Mindset	
Completion time	15 minutes

1. Log in to Server02 as **contoso\administrator** with the password of **Pa$$w0rd**.

2. Click the **File Explorer** icon on the taskbar.

3. Navigate to and open the **C:\Users** folder and then delete the **Public** folder.

4. On Server02, using Server Manager, click **Tools > Windows Server Backup**.

5. In Windows Server Backup, click **Local Backup**.

6. Under the Actions pane, click **Recover**.

7. In the Recovery Wizard, This server (Server02) is already selected. Click **Next**.

8. On the Select Backup Date page, (as shown in Figure 9-1), on the calendar, click the date of the first backup that you performed in the last lesson. Then in the Time pull-down menu, click the time of the first backup that you performed. The Location should show \\storage01\Bak\Bak1. Click **Next**.

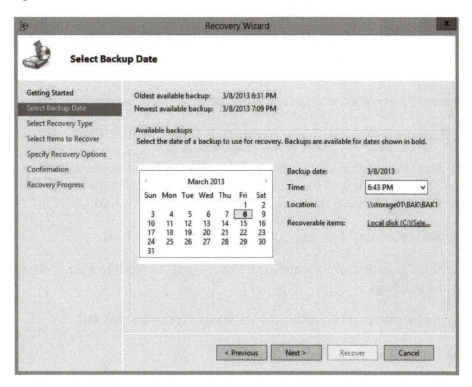

Figure 9-1
Specifying which backup to restore

9. On the Select Recovery Type page, Files and folders is already selected. Click **Next**.

10. On the Select Items to Recover page, under Available items, expand **Server02**, expand **Local disk (C:)**, expand **Users**, and then click **Public**. Click **Next**.

11. On the Specify Recovery Options page, click **Next**.

12. On the Confirmation page, click **Recover**.

13. When the files have been recovered, take a screen shot of the Properties window by pressing Alt+Prt Scr and then paste it into your Lab 9 worksheet file in the page provided by pressing Ctrl+V.

14. Click **Close**.

15. Using File Explorer, verify that the **C:\Public** folder has been restored.

16. Close **File Explorer**.

End of lab. Leave Windows Server Backup open for the next exercise.

Exercise 9.2	Restoring the System State of a System
Overview	In this exercise, you will restore the system state that was backed up during the last exercise.
Mindset	
Completion time	20 minutes

1. On Server02, using Windows Server Backup, under the Actions pane, click **Recover**.

2. In the Recovery wizard, This server (Server02) is already selected. Click **Next**.

3. On the Select Backup Date page, on the calendar, click the date of the second backup that you performed in the last lesson. Then in the Time pull-down menu, click the time of the second backup that you performed. The Location should show \\storage01\Bak\Bak2. Click **Next**.

4. On the Select Recovery Type page, click **System State**. Click **Next**.

5. On the Select Location for System State Recovery page, Original location is already selected. Click **Next**.

6. When you are prompted to confirm that you want to continue, click **OK**.

7. On the Confirmation page, click **Recover**.

8. When you are prompted to confirm that you want to continue, click **Yes**. When performing the restore, be patient. The backup will take up to 15 minutes to perform the restore, and the backup program might stop responding during this time.

9. If the computer does not reboot by itself, click **Close** and then reboot the server.

End of exercise. Close any open windows before you begin the next exercise.

Exercise 9.3	Restoring a File Using Shadow Copy
Overview	In this exercise, you will access the previous versions of files that were saved with shadow copy and then restore those files.
Mindset	
Completion time	10 minutes

1. Log in to Server01 as **contoso\administrator** with the password of **Pa$$w0rd**.

2. Click the **File Explorer** icon on the taskbar.

3. Using File Explorer, right-click the **C:\CorpDocs** folder and choose **Properties**.

4. In the Properties dialog box, click the **Previous Versions** tab (see Figure 9-2).

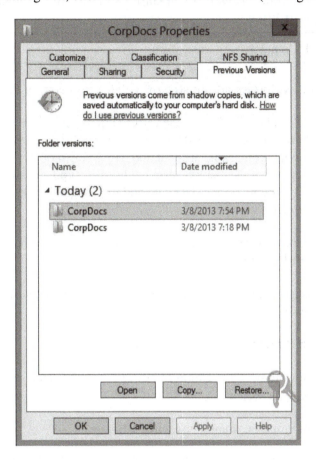

Figure 9-2
Viewing previous versions of files

5. Click the first **CorpDocs** folder and then click **Copy**.

6. In the Copy Items dialog box, click **Desktop** and then click **Copy**.

7. Click **OK** to close the CorpDocs Properties dialog box.

8. Open the **CorpDocs** folder on the Desktop and verify that the **Agenda.txt** text file is there.

9. When the file has been recovered, take a screen shot of the CorpDocs window by pressing Alt+Prt Scr and then paste it into your Lab 9 worksheet file in the page provided by pressing Ctrl+V.

10. Close the **CorpDocs** folder.

End of exercise. Close any open windows before you begin the next exercise.

Exercise 9.4	Booting into Safe Mode
Overview	In this exercise, you will boot to Safe Mode and then review the various tools that can be used to troubleshoot Windows.
Mindset	You are trying to troubleshoot a computer that will not boot Windows. How can you start Windows RE if you cannot start Windows?
Completion time	15 minutes

1. Log in to Server02 as **contoso\administrator** with the password of **Pa$$w0rd**.

2. If an error message displays, indicating the trust relationship between this workstation and the primary domain failed, it failed because the backup of the system state was done long ago and the computer machine account and its password do not match the domain database. This occurs when the machine account has been updated since the system state backup was done. Therefore, you will need to add the computer back to the domain by performing the following steps:

   a. Log in as the local **Server02\administrator** (not the contoso\administrator) with the password of **Pa$$w0rd**.

   b. When a message displays, indicating the system state has been successfully completed, press **Enter**.

   c. Right-click the **Start** button and choose **System**.

   d. In the System window, click **Change settings** in the Computer name, domain, and workgroup settings section.

   e. In the System Properties dialog box, click **Change**.

   f. In the Computer Name/Domain Changes dialog box, click **Workgroup** and then type **WG** in the Workgroup text box. Click **OK**.

   g. When a message displays, indicating you will need to know the password of the local administrator account, click **OK**.

   h. When the Welcome to the WG workgroup message appears, click **OK**.

   i. When a message displays, indicating you must restart the computer, click **OK**.

   j. In the System Properties dialog box, click **Change** again.

   k. In the Computer Name/Domain Changes dialog box, click **Domain**.

   l. In the Domain text box, type **Contoso.com** and then click **OK**.

    m. In the Windows Security dialog box, log in as **Administrator** with the password of **Pa$$w0rd**.

    n. When the Welcome to the contoso.com domain appears, click **OK**.

    o. When a message displays, indicating you must restart your computer, click **OK**.

    p. Click **Close** to close the System Properties dialog box.

    q. Click **Restart Now**.

    r. Log in as **contoso\administrator** with the password of **Pa$$w0rd**.

3. If you did not need to add the computer back to the domain, when a message displays, indicating the system state has been successfully completed, press **Enter**.

4. On Server02, execute the following command at a command prompt:

    shutdown /r /o.

5. When prompted, click **Close**. The system will shut down in less than a minute.

6. Click the **Troubleshoot** tile (as shown in Figure 9-3).

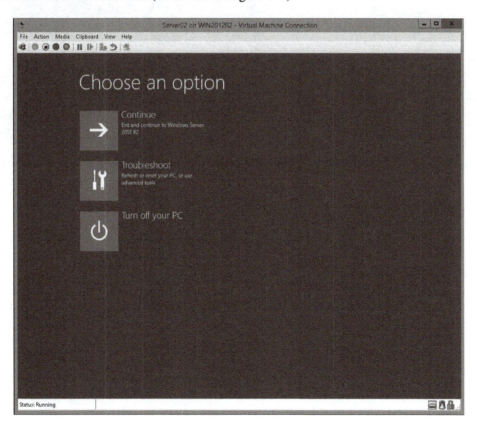

Figure 9-3
Choosing a boot option

7. Click the **Startup Settings** tile.

8. Select **Restart**.

9. In the Advanced Boot Options menu (as shown in Figure 9-4), click **Safe Mode** and then press **Enter**.

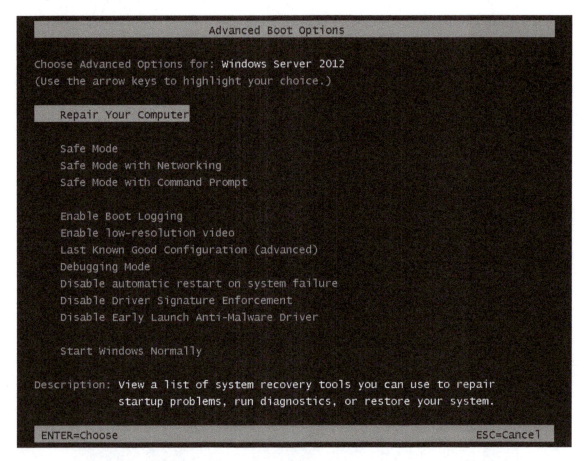

```
                        Advanced Boot Options

Choose Advanced Options for: Windows Server 2012
(Use the arrow keys to highlight your choice.)


   Repair Your Computer

   Safe Mode
   Safe Mode with Networking
   Safe Mode with Command Prompt

   Enable Boot Logging
   Enable low-resolution video
   Last Known Good Configuration (advanced)
   Debugging Mode
   Disable automatic restart on system failure
   Disable Driver Signature Enforcement
   Disable Early Launch Anti-Malware Driver


   Start Windows Normally

Description: View a list of system recovery tools you can use to repair
             startup problems, run diagnostics, or restore your system.


 ENTER=Choose                                        ESC=Cancel
```

Figure 9-4
Selecting a boot option from Advanced Boot Options

10. After Server02 reboots, log in as **contoso\administrator**.

11. Close the Windows Help and Support window.

12. Confirm your system is now in Safe Mode. The term "Safe Mode" should appear on each corner of your desktop, as shown in Figure 9-5.

Figure 9-5
Booting to Safe Mode

13. Click the **Start** button, type **msconfig**, and then click **System Configuration**.

14. Take a screen shot of the System Configuration Boot tab by pressing Alt+Prt Scr and then paste it into your Lab 9 worksheet file in the page provided by pressing Ctrl+V.

15. Click the **Boot** tab.

Question 1	What is the boot entry that you have?

16. Click the **Services** tab.

Question 2	How many services are running?

17. Click to select **Hide all Microsoft services**.

Question 3	How many non-Microsoft services do you have?

18. Click OK to close **System Configuration**.

19. Click the **Start** button, type **compmgmt.msc**, and then click **Computer Management**.

Question 4	*What did compmgmt open?*

20. Expand **Event Viewer > Windows logs** and review the **System** log and the **Application** log. If you actually had a problem, you would look for events that would help you troubleshoot the problem.

21. Close the **Computer Management** console.

22. Use File Explorer to navigate to **c:\Windows** folder and then locate the **ntbtlog.txt** file.

23. Open the **ntbtlog.txt** file and then view its contents.

24. Take a screen shot of the ntbtlog file by pressing Alt+Prt Scr and then paste it into your Lab 9 worksheet file in the page provided by pressing Ctrl+V.

25. Close the ntbtlog.txt file.

26. Use Settings in the right pop-up bar to restart the server.

End of exercise. Close any open windows before you begin the next exercise.

Exercise 9.5	Using Command Prompt Repair Tools
Overview	In this exercise, you will boot to a command prompt and then execute several command-prompt tools that can be used to fix boot problems.
Mindset	
Completion time	15 minutes

1. Log in to Server02 as **contoso\administrator** with the password of **Pa$$w0rd**.

2. On Server02, execute the following command at a command prompt:

   shutdown /r /o

3. When prompted, click **Close**. The system will shut down in less than a minute.

4. Click the **Troubleshoot** tile.

5. Click the **Command Prompt** tile.

6. Click **Administrator**.

7. In the Enter the Password for this account text box, type the **Pa$$w0rd** password and then click **Continue**.

8. At the command prompt, execute the following command:

   bootrec

9. Take a screen shot of the command prompt window by pressing Alt+Prt Scr and then paste it into your Lab 9 worksheet file in the page provided by pressing Ctrl+V.

Question 5	Which option is used to fix the boot sector?

10. At the command prompt, execute the following command:

    bootrec /FixMbr

11. Execute the following command:

    diskpart

12. At the DISKPART> command prompt, execute the following command:

    ?

13. At the DISKPART> command prompt, execute the following commands:

    list disk

    list volume

14. At the DISKPART command prompt, execute the following command:

    exit

15. The default boot time to display the boot menu on multi-boot system is 30 seconds. To change that to 10 seconds, execute the following command:

    bcdedit /timeout 10

16. To export the BcdStore to the C:\ drive, execute the following command:

    bcdedit /export C:\BcdStore

17. Execute the following command:

    bcdedit /?

Question 6	*Which option is used to change the /default operating system?*

18. To rebuild the BCD, execute the following command:

   bootrec /rebuildbcd

19. To close the command prompt, execute the following command:

   exit

20. When you are prompted to choose an option, click **Continue**.

End of exercise. Close any open windows before you begin the next exercise.

LAB REVIEW QUESTIONS

Completion time	**10 minutes**

1. In Exercise 9.1, which program is used to restore files from backup?

2. In Exercise 9.3, how are previous versions of files and folders accessed?

3. In Exercise 9.4, which command is used to reboot the computer into the Advanced Boot options menu?

4. In Exercise 9.4, which program is used to stop a service from starting during the Windows boot?

5. In Exercise 9.4, which command is used to rebuild the BCD?

Lab Challenge	Performing an Authoritative Restore
Overview	To complete this challenge, you will describe how to perform an authoritative restore.
Mindset	You need to perform an authoritative restore of Active Directory using the backup of the system state so that you can restore a user who was accidently deleted. Which steps would you need to perform to perform the authoritative restore?
Completion time	5 minutes

Write out the steps you performed to complete the challenge.

End of lab. You can log off or start a different lab. If you want to restart this lab, you'll need to click the End Lab button in order for the lab to be reset.

LAB 10
CONFIGURING SITE-LEVEL FAULT TOLERANCE

THIS LAB CONTAINS THE FOLLOWING EXERCISES AND ACTIVITIES:

Exercise 10.1   Configuring and Enabling Hyper-V Replication

Exercise 10.2   Configuring Replication for a VM

Lab Challenge   Configuring Multi-Site Failover Cluster

BEFORE YOU BEGIN

The lab environment consists of student workstations connected to a local area network, along with a server that functions as the domain controller for a domain called contoso.com. The computers required for this lab are listed in Table 10-1.

Table 10-1
Computers required for Lab 10

Computer	Operating System	Computer Name
Server (VM 1)	Windows Server 2012 R2	RWDC01
Server (VM 2)	Windows Server 2012 R2	Server01
Server (VM 3)	Windows Server 2012 R2	Server02
Server (VM 4)	Windows Server 2012 R2	Storage01

In addition to the computers, you will also require the software listed in Table 10-2 to complete Lab 10.

Table 10-2
Software required for Lab 10

Software	Location
Lab 10 student worksheet	Lab10_worksheet.docx (provided by instructor)

Working with Lab Worksheets

Each lab in this manual requires that you answer questions, shoot screen shots, and perform other activities that you will document in a worksheet named for the lab, such as Lab10_worksheet.docx. You will find these worksheets on the book companion site. It is recommended that you use a USB flash drive to store your worksheets, so you can submit them to your instructor for review. As you perform the exercises in each lab, open the appropriate worksheet file, fill in the required information, and save the file to your flash drive.

After completing this lab, you will be able to:

■ Configure and enable Hyper-V replication

■ Configure replication for a VM

■ Configure multi-site failover cluster

Estimated lab time: 65 minutes

Exercise 10.1	Configuring and Enabling Hyper-V Replication
Overview	In this exercise, you will enable Hyper-V replication on the Server01 and Server02 Hyper-V host.
Mindset	As an administrator, you want to create a backup site in case the primary site goes down. What is the best way to ensure that key virtual machines are available in the backup site?
Completion time	25 minutes

1. Log into Server01 as **contoso\administrator** with the password of **Pa$$w0rd**.

2. On Server01, in Server Manager, click **Tools > Hyper-V Manager**.

3. In the Hyper-V Manager console, right-click **Server01** and choose **Hyper-V Settings**.

4. In the Hyper-V Settings dialog box, click **Replication Configuration**.

5. In the Replication Configuration section, click to enable the **Enable this computer as a Replica server** option.

6. To enable Kerberos authentication, click to select Use **Kerberos (HTTP)**.

Question 1	What port is used with Kerberos (HTTP) authentication?

7. In the Authorization and storage section, click to select **Allow replication from any authenticated server** and then click **Browse**.

8. Navigate to the **C:** drive and click **New folder**. In the Name text box, type **VMReplica** and then press **Enter**.

9. Select the **C:\VMReplica** folder, and then click **Select Folder**.

10. Take a screen shot of the Hyper-V Settings page by pressing Alt+Prt Scr and then paste it into your Lab 10 worksheet file in the page provided by pressing Ctrl+V.

11. Click **OK** to close the Hyper-V Settings dialog box.

12. At the Inbound traffic needs to be allowed in the Firewall prompt, click **OK**.

13. Click the **Start** menu button and then click **Control Panel**.

14. In the Control Panel, click **System and Security** and then click **Windows Firewall**.

15. Click **Advanced settings**.

16. In the Windows Firewall with Advanced Security console (as shown in Figure 10-1), click **Inbound Rules**.

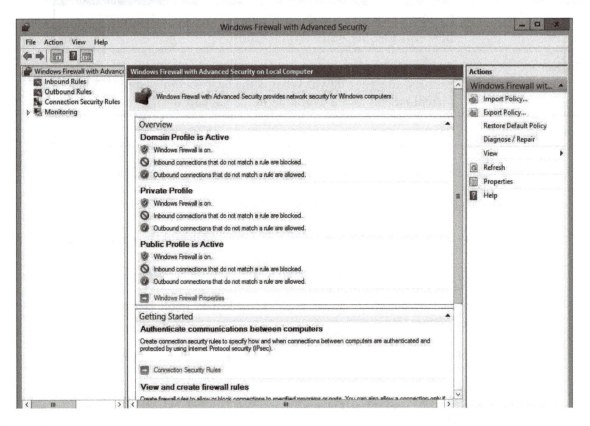

Figure 10-1
Opening Windows Firewall with Advanced Security

17. In the center pane, in the Inbound Rules list, right-click **Hyper-V Replica HTTP Listener (TCP-In)** and choose **Enable Rule**.

18. Take a screen shot of the Windows Firewall with Advanced Security console by pressing Alt+Prt Scr and then paste it into your Lab 10 worksheet file in the page provided by pressing Ctrl+V.

19. Close the Windows Firewall with Advanced Security console and then close Windows Firewall.

20. Log into Server02 as **contoso\administrator** with the password of **Pa$$w0rd**.

21. On Server02, in Server Manager, click **Tools > Hyper-V Manager**.

22. In the Hyper-V Manager console, right-click **Server02** and choose **Hyper-V Settings**.

23. In the Hyper-V Settings dialog box, click **Replication Configuration**.

24. In the Replication Configuration section, click to enable the **Enable this computer as a Replica server** option.

25. To enable Kerberos authentication, click to select **Use Kerberos (HTTP)**.

26. In the Authorization and storage section, click to select **Allow replication from any authenticated server** and then click **Browse**.

27. Navigate to the **C:** drive and click **New folder.** In the Name text box, type **VMReplica** and then press Enter.

28. Select the **C:\VMReplica** folder and then click **Select Folder**.

29. Click **OK** to close the Hyper-V Settings dialog box.

30. At the Inbound traffic needs to be allowed in the Firewall prompt, click **OK**.

31. Click the **Start** menu button and then click **Control Panel**.

32. In the Control Panel, click **System and Security** and then click **Windows Firewall**.

33. Click **Advanced settings**.

34. In the Windows Firewall with Advanced Security console, click **Inbound Rules**.

35. In the center pane, in the Inbound Rules list, right-click **Hyper-V Replica HTTP Listener (TCP-In)** and choose **Enable Rule**.

36. Close the Windows Firewall with Advanced Security console and then close Windows Firewall.

End of exercise. Leave any windows open for the next exercise.

Exercise 10.2	Configuring Replication for a VM
Overview	In this exercise, you will continue with the last exercise by configuring replication of a VM between two Hyper-V hosts.
Completion time	15 minutes

1. On Server01, using Hyper-V Manager, right-click the first **TestVM** and choose **Enable Replication**.

2. In the Enable Replication Wizard, click **Next**.

3. On the Specify Replica Server page, in the Replica server text box, type **Server02** and then click **Next**.

4. On the Specify Connection Parameters dialog box, click **Next**.

5. On the Choose Replication VHDs page, the virtual hard disk is already selected. Click **Next**.

6. On the Configure Recovery History page, the Only the latest recovery point option is already selected. Click **Next**.

7. On the Choose Initial Replication Methods page, Send initial copy over the network and Start replication immediately are already selected. Click **Next**.

8. On the Summary page, take a screen shot of the Summary page by pressing Alt+Prt Scr and then paste it into your Lab 10 worksheet file in the page provided by pressing Ctrl+V.

9. Click **Finish**.

10. Go to the **C:\VMReplica** folder on Server02 to see if the server has been replicated after a few minutes.

End of exercise. Close any open windows before you begin the next exercise.

LAB REVIEW QUESTIONS

Completion time   10 minutes

1. In Exercise 10.1, what is the first step to replicating a virtual machine from one Hyper-V host to another Hyper-V host?

2. In Exercise 10.1, for replication to function, what must be configured at the end of the exercise?

3. In Exercise 10.2, how is replication of a VM enabled?

Lab Challenge	Configuring Multi-Site Failover Cluster
Overview	To complete this challenge, you will describe how to configure multi-site failover cluster.
Mindset	You administer a corporate office in New York and a failover site in Las Vegas. What must be done to enable multi-site clustering?
Completion time	15 minutes

Write out the steps you performed to complete the challenge.

End of lab. You can log off or start a different lab. If you want to restart this lab, you'll need to click the End Lab button in order for the lab to be reset.

LAB 11
IMPLEMENTING AN ADVANCED DYNAMIC HOST CONFIGURATION PROTOCOL (DHCP) SOLUTION

THIS LAB CONTAINS THE FOLLOWING EXERCISES AND ACTIVITIES:

Exercise 11.1 Creating a Vendor Class

Exercise 11.2 Creating a DHCP Policy

Exercise 11.3 Creating and Configuring a Superscope

Exercise 11.4 Creating and Configuring Multicast Scopes

Exercise 11.5 Implementing DHCPv6 Scopes

Exercise 11.6 Configuring DHCP Name Protection

Lab Challenge Creating a DHCP Split Scope

BEFORE YOU BEGIN

The lab environment consists of student workstations connected to a local area network, along with a server that functions as the domain controller for a domain called contoso.com. The computers required for this lab are listed in Table 11-1.

Table 11-1
Computers required for Lab 11

Computer	Operating System	Computer Name
Server (VM 1)	Windows Server 2012 R2	RWDC01

In addition to the computers, you will also require the software listed in Table 11-2 to complete Lab 11.

Table 11-2
Software required for Lab 11

Software	Location
Lab 11 student worksheet	Lab11_worksheet.docx (provided by instructor)

Working with Lab Worksheets

Each lab in this manual requires that you answer questions, shoot screen shots, and perform other activities that you will document in a worksheet named for the lab, such as Lab11_worksheet.docx. You will find these worksheets on the book companion site. It is recommended that you use a USB flash drive to store your worksheets, so you can submit them to your instructor for review. As you perform the exercises in each lab, open the appropriate worksheet file, fill in the required information, and save the file to your flash drive.

After completing this lab, you will be able to:

- Create a vendor class

- Create a DHCP policy

- Create and configure a DHCP superscope

- Create and configure a multicast scope

- Implement a DHCPv6 scope

- Configure DHCP name protection

- Configure a DHCP split scope

Estimated lab time: 90 minutes

Exercise 11.1	Creating a Vendor Class
Overview	In this exercise, you will create a vendor class, which can be used when creating and defining DHCP policies.
Mindset	You have an IP phone system that you want to connect to the network. The IP phone system will have its own DHCP settings, while the computers on the subnet will have other settings. What should you do?
Completion time	10 minutes

1. Log in to RWDC01 as **contoso\administrator** with the password of **Pa$$w0rd**.

2. On RWDC01, using Server Manager, click **Tools > DHCP**. The DHCP console opens.

3. In the DHCP console, expand **rwdc01.contoso.com** and then right-click **IPv4** and choose **Define Vendor Classes...**

4. In the DHCP Vendor Classes dialog box, click **Add**. The New Class dialog box opens (see Figure 11-1).

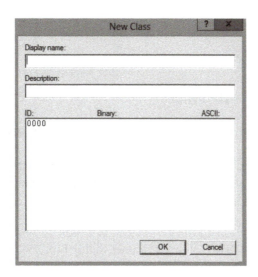

Figure 11-1
Creating a new DHCP vendor class

5. In the Display name text box, type **Nortel Phones**. In the Description text box, type **Desk phone**.

6. Click under the ASCII field name and then type **Nortel-i 2004-A**, as shown in Figure 11-2. Click **OK**.

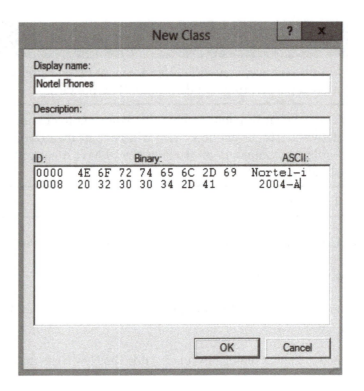

Figure 11-2
Specifying the ASCII value

7. Click **Add** again.

8. In the Display name, type **HP Printer**.

9. Click under the ASCII field and then type **Hewlett-Packard JetDirect**. Click **OK**.

10. Take a screen shot of the New Class dialog box by pressing **Alt+Prt Scr** and then paste it into your Lab 11 worksheet file in the page provided by pressing **Ctrl+V**.

11. Click **OK**.

12. Click **Close** to close the DHCP Vendor Classes dialog box.

Leave the DHCP console open for the next exercise.

Exercise 11.2	Creating a DHCP Policy
Overview	In this exercise, you will continue with the last exercise to create a DHCP scope and assign a DHCP policy to the scope.
Mindset	
Completion time	15 minutes

1. On RWDC01, using the DHCP console, right-click **IPv4** and choose **New Scope**.

2. In the New Scope Wizard, click **Next**.

3. In the Scope Name page, in the Name text box, type **NormalScope** and then click **Next**.

4. On the IP address range, type **172.24.25.50** for the Start IP address and then type **172.24.25.200** for the End IP address. For the subnet mask, type **255.255.255.0**. Click **Next**.

5. On the Add Exclusions and Delay page, click **Next**.

6. On the Lease Duration page, answer the following question and then click **Next**.

Question 1	What is the default lease duration?

7. On the Configure DHCP Options page, click **Next**.

8. On the Router (Default Gateway) page, type **172.24.25.20** for the IP address and then click **Add**. Click **Next**.

9. On the Domain Name and DNS Servers page, remove any IP addresses. Then type **192.168.1.50** in the IP address text box and click **Add**. Wait for DNS Validation. Click **Next**.

10. On the WINS Servers page, click **Next**.

11. On the Activate Scope page, click **Next**.

12. When the wizard is complete, click **Finish**.

13. Expand the IPv4 node and expand the Scope [172.24.25.0] NormalScope.

14. Under the NormalScope scope, right-click the **Policies** node and choose **New Policy**.

Question 2	Where do you define a DHCP policy?

15. In the DHCP Policy Configuration Wizard, type **Policy1** for the policy name and then click **Next**.

16. On the Configure Conditions for the policy page, click **Add**.

17. In the Add/Edit Condition dialog box, select the following (as shown in Figure 11-3) and then click **Add**:

Criteria: **Vendor Class**

Operator: **Equals**

Value: **Nortel Phones**

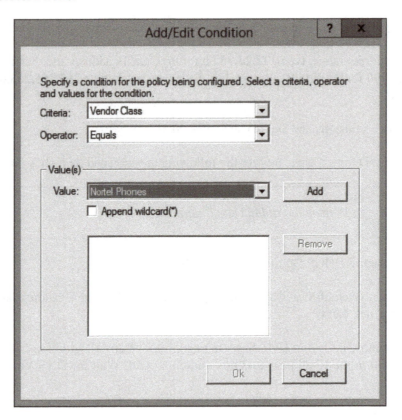

Figure 11-3
Specifying the condition used in a DHCP policy

18. Click **OK** to close the Add/Edit Condition dialog box.

19. Back on the Configure Conditions for the policy page, click **Next**.

20. On the Configure settings for the policy page, type **172.24.25.50** for the Start IP address and type **172.24.25.99** for the End IP address. Click **Next**.

21. If you need different options for the Nortel Phones, you would specify them. For now, click **Next**.

22. On the Summary page, click **Finish**.

23. Right-click **Policy1** and choose **Properties**.

24. In the Policy1 Properties dialog box, click to select the **Set lease duration for the policy** option.

25. Change the lease time to **7** days.

26. Take a screen shot of the Properties dialog box by pressing **Alt+Prt Scr** and then paste it into your Lab 11 worksheet file in the page provided by pressing **Ctrl+V**.

27. Click **OK**.

Leave the DHCP console open for the next exercise.

Exercise 11.3	Creating and Configuring a Superscope
Overview	In this exercise, you will use two normal DHCP scopes to create a superscope.
Mindset	You administer an IPv4 DHCP scope that is close to running out of addresses. How can you add more addresses to the pool that is assigned to the hosts on the subnet?
Completion time	20 minutes

1. On RWDC01, using the DHCP console, right-click **IPv4** and choose **New Scope**.

2. In the New Scope Wizard, click **Next**.

3. In the Name text box, type **Scope1** and then click **Next**.

4. In the IP address range, set the Start IP address to **172.24.20.50** and set the End IP address to **172.24.20.240**. For the Subnet mask, type **255.255.255.0**. Click **Next**.

5. On the Add Exclusions and Delay page, click **Next**.

6. On the Lease Duration page, change the duration to **3** days and then click **Next**.

7. On the Configure DHCP Options page, click **Next**.

8. On the Router (Default Gateway) page, type the address of **172.24.20.20** and then click **Add**. Click **Next**.

9. On the Domain name and DNS Servers page, the Parent domain should already be set to contoso.com. Remove the current address and then add **192.168.1.50**. Wait for DNS Validation. Click **Next**.

10. On the WINS Servers page, click **Next**.

11. On the Activate Scope page, click **Next**.

12. When the wizard is complete, click **Finish**.

13. Right-click **IPv4** and choose **New Scope**.

14. In the New Wizard, click **Next**.

15. In the Name text box, type **Scope2** and then click **Next**.

16. In the IP address range, set the Start IP address to **172.24.21.50** and set the End IP address to **172.24.21.240**. For the Subnet mask, type **255.255.255.0**. Click **Next**.

17. On the Add Exclusions and Delay page, click **Next**.

18. On the Lease Duration page, change the duration to **3** days and then click **Next**.

19. On the Configure DHCP Options, click **Next**.

20. On the Router (Default Gateway) page, type the address of **172.24.21.20** and then click **Add**. Click **Next**.

21. On the Domain name and DNS Servers page, the Parent domain should already be set to contoso.com. Remove the current address and then add **192.168.1.50**. Wait for DNS Validation. Click **Next**.

22. On the WINS Servers page, click **Next**.

23. On the Activate Scope page, click **Next**.

24. When the wizard is complete, click **Finish**.

25. Right-click **IPv4** and choose **New Superscope**.

26. In the New Superscope Wizard, click **Next**, type **Super1** in the Superscope Name text box, and then click **Next**.

27. On the Select Scopes page, press and hold the **Control key** and then click **Scope1** and **Scope2**. Release the **Control key**. When done, the Select Scopes page looks like Figure 11-4. Click **Next**.

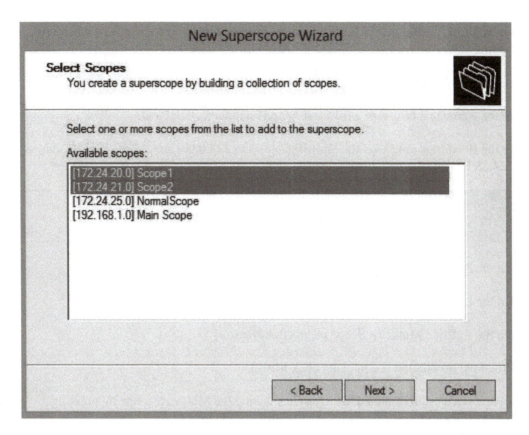

Figure 11-4
Specifying the scopes to use in a DHCP Superscope

28. Click **Finish**. The superscope shows in the DHCP console.

29. Take a screen shot of the DHCP console showing the Superscope Super1 by pressing **Alt+Prt Scr** and then paste it into your Lab 11 worksheet file in the page provided by pressing **Ctrl+V**.

Leave the DHCP console open for the next exercise.

Exercise 11.4	Creating and Configuring Multicast Scopes
Overview	In this exercise, you will create and configure a multicast scope.
Mindset	You work for a large corporation. The quarterly status meeting is shown to all employees via the corporation's various sites. What infrastructure mechanism do you need to put into place so that the video stream can be sent to all users while minimizing the traffic generated on the network?
Completion time	10 minutes

1. On RWDC01, using the DHCP console, right-click **IPv4** and choose **New Multicast Scope**.

2. In the New Multicast Scope Wizard, click **Next**.

3. In the Name text box, type **Multicast Scope1** and then click **Next**.

4. In the IP address range, set the Start IP address to **224.0.0.0** and set the End IP address to **224.255.255.255**. Click **Next**.

Question 3	To which class are multicast scopes assigned?

5. On the Add Exclusions page, click **Next**.

6. On the Lease Duration page, click **Next**.

7. On the Activate Multicast Scope page, click **Next**.

8. When the installation is complete, click **Finish**.

9. Take a screen shot of the DHCP console showing the Multicast scope by pressing **Alt+Prt Scr** and then paste it into your Lab 11 worksheet file in the page provided by pressing **Ctrl+V**.

Leave the DHCP console open for the next exercise.

Exercise 11.5	Implementing DHCPv6 Scopes
Overview	In this exercise, you will create a DHCPv6 scope.
Mindset	You are migrating your company to IPv6. Which properties must be defined when you create an IPv6 DHCP scope?
Completion time	10 minutes

1. On RWDC01, using the DHCP console, right-click **IPv6** and choose **New Scope**.

2. In the New Scope Wizard, click **Next**.

3. In the Name text box, type **IPv6Scope1**. Click **Next**.

4. On the Scope Prefix page, in the Prefix text box, type **FEC0:** (see Figure 11-5). Click **Next**.

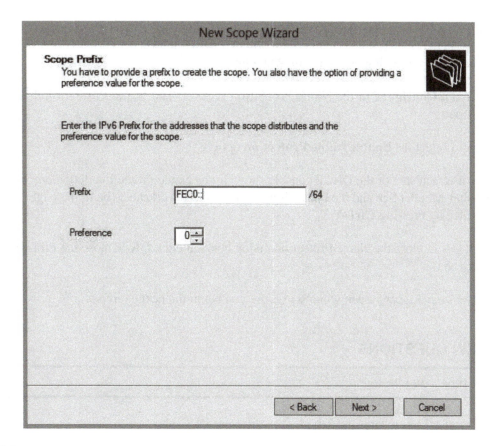

Figure 11-5
Specifying the scope prefix

> 5. On the Add Exclusions page, click **Next**.

> 6. On the Scope Lease page, change the Preferred Life Time to **1** day and change the Valid Life Time to **10** days. Click **Next**.

> 7. When the New Scope Wizard is complete, Yes is already selected to activate the scope now. Click **Finish**.

> 8. Take a screen shot of the DHCP console showing the IPv6 scope by pressing **Alt+Prt Scr** and then paste it into your Lab 11 worksheet file in the page provided by pressing **Ctrl+V**.

Leave the DHCP console open for the next exercise.

Exercise 11.6	Configuring DHCP Name Protection
Overview	In this exercise, to help protect against non-Microsoft systems from overwriting systems that use static addresses, you will enable DHCP Name Protection.
Mindset	
Completion time	5 minutes

1. On RWDC01, using the DHCP console, right-click **IPv4** and choose **Properties**.

2. In the Properties dialog box, click the **DNS** tab.

3. Click the **Configure** in the Name Protection section. The Name Protection dialog box opens.

4. Click to select the **Enable Name Protection** option.

5. Take a screen shot of the DHCP console showing the Name Protection dialog box by pressing **Alt+Prt Scr** and then paste it into your Lab 11 worksheet file in the page provided by pressing **Ctrl+V**.

6. Click **OK** to close the Name Protection dialog box and click **OK** to close the Properties dialog box.

End of exercise. Close any open windows before you begin the next exercise.

LAB REVIEW QUESTIONS

Completion time   10 minutes

1. In Exercise 11.1, what is used to identify different DHCP hosts?

2. In Exercise 11.2, what created a DHCP policy and what was used to determine if a policy would be applied to a host?

3. In Exercise 11.4, what is the beginning address of the multiscope address that you can assign?

4. In Exercise 11.5, how many bits are used in an IPv6 address?

5. In Exercise 11.5, how many bits are used for the network bits of the IPv6 scope?

6. In Exercise 11.6, on which tab are the DHCP Name Protection settings found?

Lab Challenge	Creating a DHCP Split Scope
Overview	To complete this challenge, you will describe how to create a DHCP split scope.
Mindset	You decide to use two DHCP servers. The primary DHCP server will house 80 percent of the addresses and the secondary DHCP server will house 20 percent of the addresses. How would you configure the address split?
Completion time	10 minutes

Write out the steps you performed to complete the challenge.

End of lab. You can log off or start a different lab. If you want to restart this lab, you'll need to click the End Lab button in order for the lab to be reset.

LAB 12
IMPLEMENTING AN ADVANCED DNS SOLUTION

THIS LAB CONTAINS THE FOLLOWING EXERCISES AND ACTIVITIES:

- -

Exercise 12.1   Configuring DNSSEC

Exercise 12.2   Enabling DNS Cache Locking

Exercise 12.3   Configuring DNS Logging

Exercise 12.4   Disabling Recursion

Exercise 12.5   Configuring Netmask Ordering

Exercise 12.6   Configuring a GlobalNames Zone

Lab Challenge   Delegating DNS Administration

BEFORE YOU BEGIN

The lab environment consists of student workstations connected to a local area network, along with a server that functions as the domain controller for a domain called contoso.com. The computers required for this lab are listed in Table 12-1.

Table 12-1
Computers required for Lab 12

Computer	Operating System	Computer Name
Server (VM 1)	Windows Server 2012 R2	RWDC01

In addition to the computers, you will also require the software listed in Table 12-2 to complete Lab 12.

Table 12-2
Software required for Lab 12

Software	Location
Lab 12 student worksheet	Lab12_worksheet.docx (provided by instructor)

Working with Lab Worksheets

Each lab in this manual requires that you answer questions, shoot screen shots, and perform other activities that you will document in a worksheet named for the lab, such as Lab12_worksheet.docx. You will find these worksheets on the book companion site. It is recommended that you use a USB flash drive to store your worksheets, so you can submit them to your instructor for review. As you perform the exercises in each lab, open the appropriate worksheet file, fill in the required information, and save the file to your flash drive.

After completing this lab, you will be able to:

■ Configure security for DNSSEC and cache locking

■ Configure DNS logging

■ Disable DNS recursion

■ Configure netmask ordering

■ Enable and configure a GlobalNames zone

■ Delegate DNS administration

Estimated lab time: 75 minutes

Exercise 12.1	Configuring DNSSEC
Overview	In this exercise, you will configure DNSSEC for a DNS zone.
Mindset	What resource records are created when you sign a zone?
Completion time	15 minutes

1. Log in to RWDC01 as **contoso\administrator** with the password of **Pa$$w0rd**.

2. In Server Manager, click **Tools > DNS**.

3. In the DNS console, expand **RWDC01 (if necessary)** and then expand **Forward Lookup Zones**.

4. Right-click the **Contoso.com** zone and choose **DNSSEC > Sign the Zone**.

5. In the Zone Signing Wizard, click **Next**.

6. On the Signing Options page, ensure Customize zone signing parameters is selected and then click **Next**.

7. On the Key Master page, click **Next**.

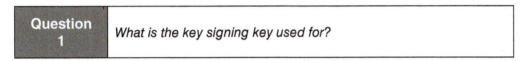

Question 1	*What is the key signing key used for?*

8. On the Key Signing Key (KSK) page, click **Next**.

9. In the Key Signing Key (KSK) dialog box (see Figure 12-1), click **Add**.

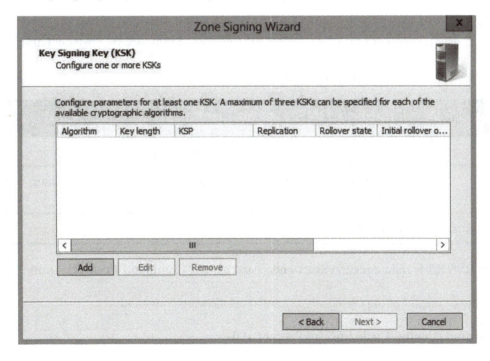

Figure 12-1
Configuring the key signing key

10. In the New Key Signing Key (KSK) dialog box, click **OK**.

11. Back on the Key Signing Key (KSK) page, click **Next**.

Question 2	What is the zone signing key used for?

12. On the Zone Signing Key (ZSK) page, click **Next**.

13. In the Zone Signing Key (ZSK) dialog box, click **Add**.

14. In the New Zone Signing Key (ZSK) dialog box, click **OK**.

15. Back on the Zone Signing Key (ZSK) page, click **Next**.

16. On the Next Secure (NSEC) page, click **Next**.

17. On the Trust Anchors (TAs) page, click **Next**.

18. On the Signing and Polling Parameters page, click **Next**.

19. On the DNS Security Extension (DNSSEC) page, click **Next**.

20. When the zone has been successfully signed, click **Finish**.

21. With the contoso.com domain highlighted, press the **F5** key to refresh the list.

22. Take a screen shot of the DNS Manager console window by pressing **Alt+Prt Scr** and then paste it into your Lab 12 worksheet file in the page provided by pressing **Ctrl+V**.

Leave the DNS console open for later exercises.

Exercise 12.2	Enabling DNS Cache Locking
Overview	In this exercise, you will enable DNS cache locking.
Mindset	When you configure DNS Cache locking, what is the optimum setting?
Completion time	10 minutes

1. On RWDC01, right-click the **Start** button and choose **Command Prompt (Admin)**.

2. In the command prompt window, execute the following command:

   Dnscmd /Config /CacheLockingPercent 100

3. Execute the following command:

   Net stop DNS

4. Execute the following command:

   Net start DNS

5. Take a screen shot of the Command Prompt window by pressing **Alt+Prt Scr** and then paste it into your Lab 12 worksheet file in the page provided by pressing **Ctrl+V**.

6. Close the Command prompt window.

End of exercise. Close any open windows before you begin the next exercise.

Exercise 12.3	Configuring DNS Logging
Overview	In this exercise, you will enable DNS Debug Logging.
Mindset	
Completion time	5 minutes

1. On RWDC01, using the DNS Manager console, right-click the **RWDC01** server and choose **Properties**.

2. In the Properties dialog box, click the **Debug Logging** tab.

3. Click to enable **Log Packets for debugging** check box.

Question 3	Which packets based on packet content are logged?

4. Take a screen shot of the DNS Manager console with the RWDC01 Properties dialog box by pressing **Alt+Prt Scr** and then paste it into your Lab 12 worksheet file in the page provided by pressing **Ctrl+V**.

5. Click **OK** to close the Properties dialog box.

6. Leave the DNS console open for the next exercise.

Exercise 12.4	Disabling Recursion
Overview	In this exercise, you will disable recursion.
Mindset	
Completion time	5 minutes

1. On RWDC01, using the DNS Manager console, right-click the **RWDC01** server and choose **Properties**.

2. In the Properties dialog, click the **Advanced** tab.

3. Click to select the **Disable recursion** check box.

Question 4	*What else gets disabled when you disable recursion?*

4. Take a screen shot of the DNS Manager console with the RWDC01 Properties dialog box by pressing **Alt+Prt Scr** and then paste it into your Lab 12 worksheet file in the page provided by pressing **Ctrl+V**.

5. Click **OK** to close the Properties dialog box.

Leave the DNS console open for next exercises.

Exercise 12.5	Configuring Netmask Ordering
Overview	In this exercise, will configure netmask ordering.
Mindset	You administer three sites with three web servers (one located at each site), each responding to the same name. You want to ensure that when users visit the website by name, the user will connect to the local web server. What option would you enable?
Completion time	5 minutes

1. On RWDC01, using the DNS Manager console, right-click the **RWDC01** server and choose **Properties**.

2. In the Properties dialog, click the **Advanced** tab.

3. Make sure that the **Enable netmask ordering** check box is enabled.

4. Click **OK** to close the Properties dialog box.

Leave the DNS console open for the next exercise.

Exercise 12.6	Configuring a GlobalNames Zone
Overview	In this exercise, you will enable and configure GlobalNames Zone to provide single name support.
Mindset	What service is GlobalNames designed to replace?
Completion time	15 minutes

1. On RWDC01, right-click the **Start** button and choose **Command Prompt (Admin)**.

2. In the command prompt window, execute the following command:

   dnscmd rwdc01 /Config /EnableGlobalnamessupport 1

3. Take a screen shot of the Command Prompt window by pressing **Alt+Prt Scr** and then paste it into your Lab 12 worksheet file in the page provided by pressing **Ctrl+V**.

4. Close the command window.

5. On RWDC01, using the DNS Manager console, right-click **RWDC01** and choose **New Zone**.

6. In the New Zone wizard, click **Next**.

7. On the Zone Type page, click **Next**.

8. On the Active Directory Zone Replication scope, click **Next**.

9. On the Forward or Reverse Lookup Zone page, click **Next**.

10. On the Zone Name page, in the Zone name text box, type **GlobalNames** and then click **Next**.

11. On the Dynamic Update page, select **Do not allow dynamic updates** and then click **Next**.

12. When the wizard is complete, click **Finish**.

13. Right-click the **GlobalNames** zone and choose **New Host (A or AAAA)**.

14. In the Name text box, type **Server01**.

15. In the IP address text box, type **192.168.1.60**.

16. Click the **Add Host** button.

17. When the record is created, click **OK**.

18. Click **Done** to close the New Host dialog box.

19. On RWDC01, right-click the **Start** button and choose **Command Prompt (Admin)**.

20. In the command prompt window, execute the following command:

    ping server01

Question 5	*What name and address did it ping?*

21. In the command prompt window, execute the following command:

    ping server01. /4

Question 6	*What name and address did it ping?*

22. Close the command prompt window.

23. Close the DNS Manager window.

End of exercise. Close any open windows before you begin the next exercise.

LAB REVIEW QUESTIONS

Completion time   10 minutes

1. In Exercise 12.1, what did you configure to allow DNS clients with proof of identity of DNS records and verified denial of existence?

2. In Exercise 12.1, what were the two types of keys that you and create when using DNSSEC?

3. In Exercise 12.2, how did you configure DNS cache locking?

4. In Exercise 12.3, how did you enable and configure DNS Logging?

5. In Exercise 12.6, how did you enable GlobalNames support?

Lab Challenge	Delegating DNS Administration
Overview	To complete this challenge, you will describe how to delegate DNS Administration by writing the steps for the following scenario.
Mindset	You want to grant DNS control to the help desk for the company DNS forward lookup zone. How can you grant access to help desk personnel without granting access to all DNS zones?
Completion time	10 minutes

Write out the steps you performed to complete the challenge.

End of lab. You can log off or start a different lab. If you want to restart this lab, you'll need to click the End Lab button in order for the lab to be reset.

LAB 13
DEPLOYING AND MANAGING IPAM

THIS LAB CONTAINS THE FOLLOWING EXERCISES AND ACTIVITIES:

Exercise 13.1   Installing an IPAM on a Member Server

Exercise 13.2   Configuring IPAM

Lab Challenge   Migrating to IPAM

BEFORE YOU BEGIN

The lab environment consists of student workstations connected to a local area network, along with a server that functions as the domain controller for a domain called contoso.com. The computers required for this lab are listed in Table 13-1.

Table 13-1
Computers required for Lab 13

Computer	Operating System	Computer Name
Server (VM 1)	Windows Server 2012 R2	RWDC01
Server (VM 2)	Windows Server 2012 R2	Server01

In addition to the computers, you will also require the software listed in Table 13-2 to complete Lab 13.

Table 13-2
Software required for Lab 13

Software	Location
Lab 13 student worksheet	Lab13_worksheet.docx (provided by instructor)

Working with Lab Worksheets

Each lab in this manual requires that you answer questions, shoot screen shots, and perform other activities that you will document in a worksheet named for the lab, such as Lab13_worksheet.docx. You will find these worksheets on the book companion site. It is recommended that you use a USB flash drive to store your worksheets, so you can submit them to your instructor for review. As you perform the exercises in each lab, open the appropriate worksheet file, fill in the required information, and save the file to your flash drive.

After completing this lab, you will be able to:

■ Install IPAM

■ Configure IPAM

■ Migrate to IPAM

Estimated lab time: 50 minutes

Exercise 13.1	Installing IPAM on a Member Server
Overview	In this exercise, you will install the IPAM feature on a server.
Mindset	What tool was added to Windows Server 2012 R2 to plan, manage, track and audit IP addresses?
Completion time	10 minutes

1. Log in to Server01 as **contoso\administrator** with the password of **Pa$$w0rd**.

2. Using the Server Manager console, click **Manage > Add Roles and Features**.

3. In the Add Roles and Features Wizard, click **Next**.

4. On the Select installation type page, click **Next**.

5. On the Select destination server page, click **Server01.contoso.com** and then click **Next**.

6. On the Select server roles page, click **Next**.

7. On the Select features page, click to select **IP Address Management (IPAM) Server**. When you are prompted to add additional features, click **Add Features**.

8. Back on the Select features page, click **Next**.

9. On the Confirm installation selections page, click **Install**.

10. Take a screen shot of the IPAM installation by pressing Alt+Prt Scr and then paste it into your Lab 13 worksheet file in the page provided by pressing Ctrl+V.

11. When the installation is complete, click **Close**.

End of exercise. Leave Server Manager open for the next exercise.

Exercise 13.2	Configuring IPAM
Overview	In this exercise, you will configure and enable IPAM so that it can scan and manage IP addresses.
Mindset	To plan, manage, track and audit IP addresses, what servers must be accessed to gather the necessary information?
Completion time	40 minutes

1. On Server01, open Windows PowerShell by clicking the **Windows PowerShell** icon on the taskbar.

2. Execute the following command on the Windows PowerShell window:

   **Invoke-IpamGpoProvisioning–Domain contoso.com
   –GpoPrefixName IPAM1–IpamServerFqdn server01.contoso.com**

   When you are prompted to confirm this action, type **Y** and press **Enter**.

3. Close the **Windows PowerShell** window.

4. On Server01, using Server Manager, click **IPAM**. If IPAM is not shown, press the **F5** key. The IPAM overview is displayed as shown in Figure 13-1.

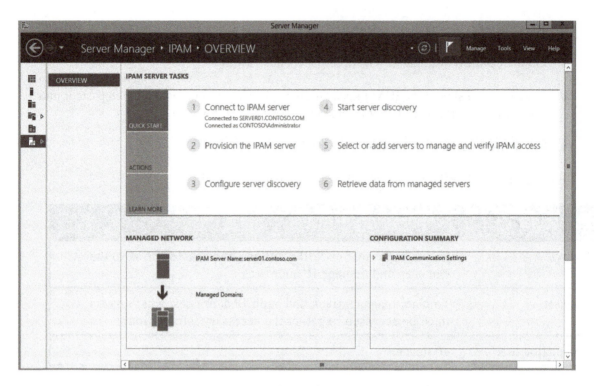

Figure 13-1
Viewing the IPAM Overview

5. Since the IPAM server is already connected to Server01, click step 2, **Provision the IPAM server**.

6. When the Provision IPAM wizard starts, click **Next**.

7. On the Configure database page, click **Next**.

8. On the Select provisioning method page, Group Policy Based is already selected. In the GPO name prefix text box, type **IPAM1** and then click **Next**.

9. On the Summary page, click **Apply**.

10. When IPAM has been provisioned, click **Close**.

11. Log in to RWDC01 as **contoso\administrator** with the password of **Pa$$w0rd**.

12. On RWDC01, in Server Manager, click **Tools > Group Policy Management**.

13. In the Group Policy Management console, expand **Forest: contoso.com**, expand **Domains**, and then expand **contoso.com**.

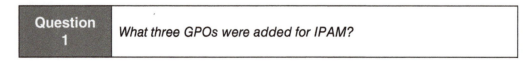

Question 1	*What three GPOs were added for IPAM?*

14. Close the **Group Policy Management** console.

15. On RWDC01, in Server Manager, click **Tools > Active Directory Users and Computers**.

16. Expand **contoso.com** and then click the **Users** container.

17. Double-click the **IPAMUG** group.

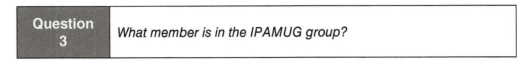

Question 2	*What type of group is IPAMUG?*

18. Click the **Members** tab.

Question 3	*What member is in the IPAMUG group?*

19. Click the **Member Of** tab.

20. Click the **Add** button. In the text box, type **Enterprise admin; Event Log Readers** and then click **OK**. Click **OK** to close IPAMUG Properties.

21. Close **Active Directory Users and Computers**.

22. Reboot RWDC01. Wait until RWDC01 finishes booting.

23. On Server01, on the IPAM Overview screen, click step 3: **Configure server discovery**.

24. In the Configure Server Discovery dialog box, the root domain (contoso.com) is already selected. Click **Add**. The Configure Server Discovery dialog box opens.

25. Click **OK** to close the Configure Server Discovery dialog box.

26. On the IPAM Overview screen, click step 4: **Start server discovery**. Wait until Server Discovery is done. At the bottom of the screen, under Scheduled Tasks, (as shown in Figure 13-2), its status should display Ready. This might take 5-10 minutes.

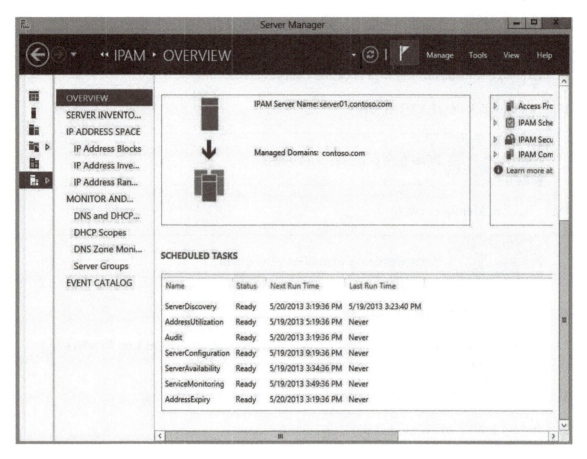

Figure 13-2
Viewing the IPAM scheduled tasks

27. On the IPAM Overview screen, click step 5: **Select or add servers to manage and verify IPAM access**.

28. On the IPv4 page, rwdc01 is blocked. Right-click **RWDC01** and choose **Edit Server**.

29. On the Add or Edit Server page, change the Manageability status Unspecified to **Managed**. Also, make sure **DC**, **DNS server**, and **DHCP server** are selected. Click **OK**.

30. Right-click the **RWDC01** server and choose **Refresh Server Access Status**.

    If a status dialog box is displayed, click **OK**. When the list is refreshed, click **F5** key to refresh the screen. If the IPAM Access is Blocked, right-click the **RWDC01** server and choose **Retrieve All Server Data**. When the retrieve all server data is complete (after a couple of minutes), right-click **RWDC01** and choose **Refresh Server Access Status** once more, followed by pressing **F5** again. By then, RWDC01 should indicate the IPAM Access Status is Unblocked, as shown in Figure 13-3.

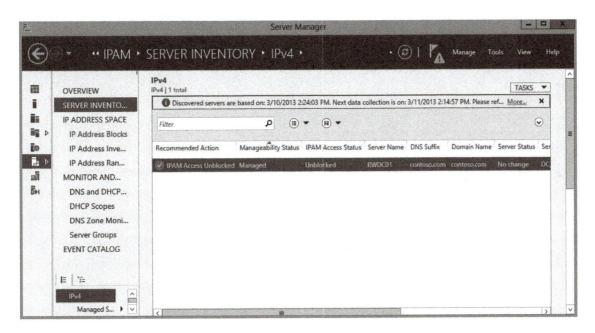

Figure 13-3
Showing RWDC01 is Unblocked

31. Take a screen shot of the IPv4 page of IPAM by pressing Alt+Prt Scr and then paste it into your Lab 13 worksheet file in the page provided by pressing Ctrl+V.

32. Click **Overview** again in the left pane.

33. Click Step 6: **Retrieve data from managed servers**. Again, this might take a couple of minutes.

34. Using Server Manager, under IP ADDRESS SPACE, click **IPAM > IP Address Blocks**.

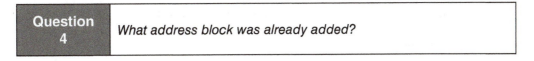

Question 4	What address block was already added?

35. Click **Tasks > Add IP Address Range**. The Add or Edit IPv4 Address Range dialog box opens.

36. Complete the dialog box fields with the required Basic IP Range configuration data using the following information and then click **OK**.

Network ID: **192.168.1.0**

Prefix length: **24**

37. Under IP ADDRESS SPACE, click **IP Address Inventory**, which is shown in Figure 13-4.

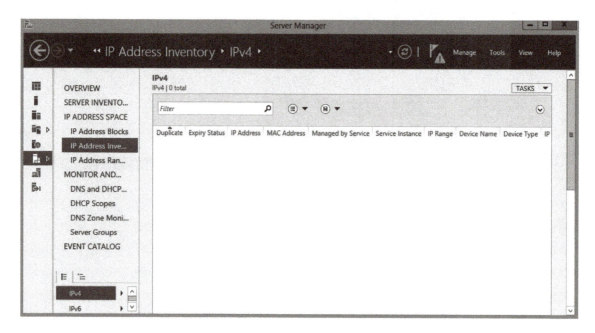

Figure 13-4
Viewing IP address inventory

38. Click **Tasks > Retrieve Address Space Data**. Wait until the task completes.

39. Under MONITOR AND MANAGE, click **DNS and DHCP Servers**.

40. Under MONITOR AND MANAGE, click **DHCP Scopes**.

41. Take a screen shot of the DHCP Scopes > IPv4 page of IPAM by pressing Alt+Prt Scr and then paste it into your Lab 13 worksheet file in the page provided by pressing Ctrl+V.

42. Under MONITOR AND MANAGE, click **DNS Zone Monitoring**.

43. Close **Server Manager**.

End of exercise. Close any open windows before you begin the next exercise.

LAB REVIEW QUESTIONS

Completion time	5 minutes

1. In Exercise 13.1, is IPAM a role or is it a feature?

2. In Exercise 13.2, besides running provisioning IPAM, how did you provision the GPOs?

3. In Exercise 13.2, which group is used to manage the resources of IPAM?

4. In Exercise 13.2, what information is retrieved when IPAM is configured?

Lab Challenge	Migrating to IPAM
Overview	To complete this challenge, you will describe how to migrate to IPAM.
Mindset	You have installed and configured IPAM, including performing the provisioning and discovery. What must be done in order to import IP address data from spreadsheets and text files?
Completion time	5 minutes

Write out the steps you performed to complete the challenge.

End of lab. You can log off or start a different lab. If you want to restart this lab, you'll need to click the End Lab button in order for the lab to be reset.

LAB 14
CONFIGURING A DOMAIN AND FOREST

THIS LAB CONTAINS THE FOLLOWING EXERCISES AND ACTIVITIES:

Exercise 14.1   Creating a Child Domain

Exercise 14.2   Demoting a Domain Controller

Exercise 14.3   Installing a New Forest

Exercise 14.4   Raising the Domain and Forest Functional Level

Exercise 14.5   Configuring Multiple UPN Suffixes

Lab Challenge   Performing an Upgrade Installation

BEFORE YOU BEGIN

The lab environment consists of student workstations connected to a local area network, along with a server that functions as the domain controller for a domain called contoso.com. The computers required for this lab are listed in Table 14-1.

Table 14-1
Computers required for Lab 14

Computer	Operating System	Computer Name
Server (VM 1)	Windows Server 2012 R2	RWDC01
Server (VM 4)	Windows Server 2012 R2	Storage01

In addition to the computers, you will also require the software listed in Table 14-2 to complete Lab 14.

Table 14-2
Software required for Lab 14

Software	Location
Lab 14 student worksheet	Lab14_worksheet.docx (provided by instructor)

Working with Lab Worksheets

Each lab in this manual requires that you answer questions, shoot screen shots, and perform other activities that you will document in a worksheet named for the lab, such as Lab14_worksheet.docx. You will find these worksheets on the book companion site. It is recommended that you use a USB flash drive to store your worksheets, so you can submit them to your instructor for review. As you perform the exercises in each lab, open the appropriate worksheet file, fill in the required information, and save the file to your flash drive.

After completing this lab, you will be able to:

■ Create a new child domain

■ Demote a domain controller

■ Install a new forest

■ Upgrade the domain and forest functional level

■ Configure multiple UPN suffixes

■ Perform an upgrade installation

Estimated lab time: 90 minutes

Exercise 14.1	Creating a Child Domain
Overview	In this exercise, you will use the Storage01 server to create a child domain that is placed under contoso.com.
Mindset	How do users from a child domain access resources on a parent domain?
Completion time	30 minutes

1. Log in to Storage01 as **contoso\administrator** with the password of **Pa$$w0rd**.

2. Click the **Start** button and then click **Control Panel**.

3. In the Control Panel, click **System and Security**.

4. Under System, click **See the name of this computer**.

5. On the System page, click **Change settings**.

6. In the System Properties dialog box, click **Change**.

7. In the Computer Name/Domain Changes dialog box, click **Workgroup** and then type **Workgroup** in the text box. Click **OK**.

8. When you are prompted to confirm that you want to continue, click **OK**.

9. When a welcome to the WORKGROUP workgroup message appears, click **OK**.

10. Click **OK** to restart the computer.

11. Click **Close** on the System Properties dialog box.

12. When a message appears, indicating that you must restart your computer to apply these changes, click **Restart Now**.

13. Log in to Storage01 as local **administrator** with the password of **Pa$$w0rd**.

14. In Server Manager, click **Manage > Add Roles and Features**.

15. In the Add Roles and Features Wizard, click **Next**.

16. On the Select installation type page, click **Next**.

17. On the Select destination server page, click **Next**.

18. On the Select server roles page, click **Active Directory Domain Services**. When you are prompted to add some features, click **Add Features**.

19. Back on the Select server roles page, click **Next**.

20. On the Select features page, click **Next**.

21. On the Active Directory Domain Services page, click **Next**.

22. On the Confirm installation selections page, click **Install**.

23. When Active Directory Domain Services is installed, click **Close**.

24. In Server Manager, click the yellow triangle with the black exclamation point and then click **Promote this server to a domain controller**.

25. In the Active Directory Domain Services Configuration Wizard, on the Deployment Configuration page, click **Add a new domain to an existing forest**.

26. In the Parent domain name text box, type **contoso.com**.

27. In the New domain name text box, type **Child**.

28. Click the **Change** button. When prompted for the username credentials, type **contoso\administrator** and **Pa$$w0rd**. Click **OK** and then click **Next**.

29. On the Domain Controllers Options page, type **Pa$$w0rd** in the Password text box and the Confirm password text box. Click **Next**.

30. On the DNS Options page, answer the following question and then click **Next**.

Question 1	*What option is already selected?*

31. On the Additional Options page, after CHILD appears in the NetBIOS domain name text box, click **Next**.

32. On the Paths page, click **Next**.

33. On the Review Options page, answer the following question and then click **Next**.

Question 2	*What roles will this server have?*

34. On the Prerequisites Check page, click **Install**.

35. On Storage01, when Windows reboots, log in as **child\administrator** with the password of **Pa$$w0rd**.

36. In Server Manager, click **Tools > Active Directory Users and Computers**.

37. In the Active Directory Users and Computers console, right-click **Child.contoso.com** and choose **Raise domain functional level**. The Raise domain functional level dialog box opens.

Question 3	*What domain functional level is the child domain and why was it set at that level?*

38. Click **Close** to close the Raise domain functional level dialog box.

39. Close **Active Directory Users and Computers**.

End of exercise. Leave Server Manager open for the next exercise.

Exercise 14.2	Demoting a Domain Controller
Overview	In this exercise, you will demote the Storage01 domain controller so that you can use it in future exercises.
Mindset	
Completion time	10 minutes

1. On Storage01, using Server Manager, click **Manage > Remove Roles and Features**.

2. In the Remove Roles and Features wizard, click **Next**.

3. On the Server destination server page, click **Next**.

4. On the Remove server roles, deselect **Active Directory Domain Services**. When a message displays, indicating that you have to remove features, click **Remove Features**.

5. In the Validation Results dialog box (as shown in Figure 14-1), click **Demote this domain controller**.

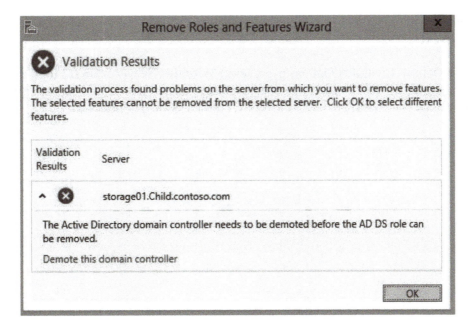

Figure 14-1
Demoting a domain controller

6. On the Credentials page, click to select **Force the removal of this domain controller** and then click **Next**.

7. When it a message displays, indicating that the current roles include Domain Name System (DNS) Server and Global Catalogs, click to select **Proceed with removal** and then click **Next**.

8. On the New Administrator Password page, type **Pa$$w0rd** in the Password text box and the Confirm password text box. Click **Next**.

9. On the Remove options page, click **Demote**. Windows will reboot when done.

End of exercise. Close any open windows before you begin the next exercise.

Exercise 14.3	Installing a New Forest
Overview	In this exercise, you will create a new forest and domain called adatum.com using Storage01.
Mindset	
Completion time	10 minutes

1. Log in to Storage01 as **administrator** with the password of **Pa$$w0rd**.

2. In Server Manager, click the yellow triangle with the black exclamation point and then click **Promote this server to a domain controller**.

3. On the Deployment Configuration, click **Add a new forest**.

4. On the Root domain name, in the Root domain name text box, type **adatum.com**. Click **Next**.

5. On the Domain Controller Options page, select **Windows Server 2008 R2** for the Forest function level and the domain functional level, as shown in Figure 14-2. In the Password text box and the Confirm password text box, type **Pa$$w0rd**. Click **Next**.

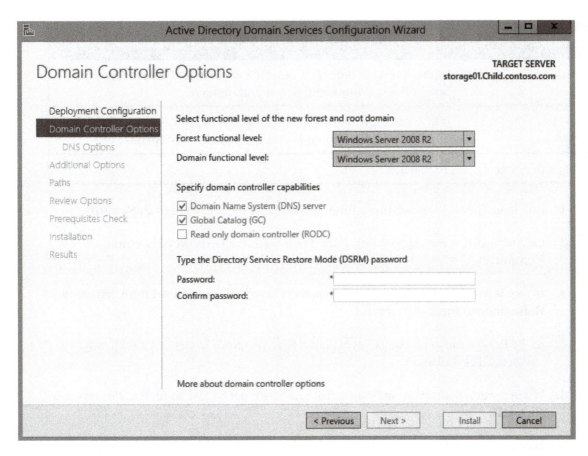

Figure 14-2
Configuring the functional level for a domain and forest

6. On the DNS Options page, click **Next**.

7. On the Additional Options page, click **Next**.

8. On the Paths page, click **Next**.

9. On the Review Options page, take a screen shot by pressing **Alt+Prt Scr** and then paste it into your Lab 14 worksheet file in the page provided by pressing **Ctrl+V**.

10. Click **Next**.

11. On the Prerequisites page, click **Install**. After a few minutes, Windows will reboot.

End of exercise. Close any open windows before you begin the next exercise.

Exercise 14.4	Raising the Domain and Forest Functional Level
Overview	In this exercise, you will raise the domain and forest functional level of the adatum.com forest and domain.
Mindset	If you have a forest functional level Windows Server 2008 R2, what domain functional levels can exist on the forest?
Completion time	10 minutes

1. Log in to Storage01 as **adatum\administrator** with the password of **Pa$$w0rd**.

2. On Storage01, in Server Manager, click **Tools > Active Directory Users and Computers**.

3. In the Active Directory Users and Computers console, right-click **Adatum** and choose **Raise domain functional level**.

4. In the Raise domain functional level dialog box, Windows Server 2012 is already selected. Click **Raise**.

5. When a warning displays, indicating that you might not be able to reverse this process, click **OK**.

6. When the functional level has been raised, take a screen shot by pressing **Alt+Prt Scr** and then paste it into your Lab 14 worksheet file in the page provided by pressing **Ctrl+V**.

7. Click **OK**.

8. Close **Active Directory users and Computers**.

9. In Server Manager, click **Tools > Active Directory Domains and Trusts**.

10. In the Active Directory Domains and Trusts console, right-click **Active Directory Domains and Trusts** and choose **Raise Forest Functional Level**.

11. In the Raise forest functional level dialog box, Windows Server 2012 R2 is already selected. Click **Raise**.

12. When a warning displays, indicating that you might not be able to reverse the process, click **OK**.

13. When the functional level has been raised, take a screen shot by pressing **Alt+Prt Scr** and then paste it into your Lab 14 worksheet file in the page provided by pressing **Ctrl+V**.

14. Click **OK**.

15. Close **Active Directory Domains and Trusts**.

End of exercise. Close any open windows before you begin the next exercise.

Exercise 14.5	Configuring Multiple UPN Suffixes
Overview	In this exercise, you will create define multiple UPN suffixes so that different logins can be used with the same user.
Mindset	What are the two formats that a user can use when logging in?
Completion time	10 minutes

1. On Storage01, in Server Manager, click **Tools > Active Directory Domains and Trusts**.

2. Right-click **Active Directory Domains and Trusts** and choose **Properties**.

3. In the Alternative UPN suffixes text box (see Figure 14-3), type **litware.com** and then click **Add**.

Figure 14-3
Configuring the UPN suffixes

4. In the Alternative UPN suffixes text box, type **adatum.contoso.com** and then click **Add**.

5. Take a screen shot of the UPN Suffixes tab by pressing **Alt+Prt Scr** and then paste it into your Lab 14 worksheet file in the page provided by pressing **Ctrl+V**.

6. Click **OK**.

7. Close **Active Directory Domains and Trusts**.

End of exercise. Close any open windows before you begin the next exercise.

LAB REVIEW QUESTIONS

Completion time   10 minutes

1. In Exercise 14.1, how did you promote a member server to a domain controller?

2. In Exercise 14.2, how did you demote a domain controller to a member server?

3. In Exercise 14.3, which forest functional levels were available?

4. In Exercise 14.4, which tool did you use to raise the domain functional level?

5. In Exercise 14.4, which tool did you use to raise the forest functional level?

6. In Exercise 14.5, which tool did you use to add alternative UPN suffixes?

Lab Challenge	Performing an Upgrade Installation
Overview	To complete this challenge, you will describe how to perform an upgrade installation by writing the steps for the following scenario.
Mindset	You administer a server and domain controller running Windows Server 2008 R2. You want to upgrade to Windows Server 2012 R2. How would you perform the upgrade?
Completion time	10 minutes

Write out the steps you performed to complete the challenge.

End of lab. You can log off or start a different lab. If you want to restart this lab, you'll need to click the End Lab button in order for the lab to be reset.

LAB 15
CONFIGURING TRUSTS

THIS LAB CONTAINS THE FOLLOWING EXERCISES AND ACTIVITIES:

Exercise 15.1   Creating and Configuring a One-Way External Trust

Exercise 15.2   Creating and Configuring a Two-Way Forest Trust

Exercise 15.3   Validating and Testing a Trust

Lab Challenge   Configuring Selective Authorization between two Trusted Domains

BEFORE YOU BEGIN

The lab environment consists of student workstations connected to a local area network, along with a server that functions as the domain controller for a domain called contoso.com. The computers required for this lab are listed in Table 15-1.

Table 15-1
Computers required for Lab 15

Computer	Operating System	Computer Name
Server (VM 1)	Windows Server 2012 R2	RWDC01
Server (VM 4)	Windows Server 2012 R2	Storage01

In addition to the computers, you will also require the software listed in Table 15-2 to complete Lab 15.

Table 15-2
Software required for Lab 15

Software	Location
Lab 15 student worksheet	Lab15_worksheet.docx (provided by instructor)

Working with Lab Worksheets

Each lab in this manual requires that you answer questions, shoot screen shots, and perform other activities that you will document in a worksheet named for the lab, such as Lab15_worksheet.docx. You will find these worksheets on the book companion site. It is recommended that you use a USB flash drive to store your worksheets, so you can submit them to your instructor for review. As you perform the exercises in each lab, open the appropriate worksheet file, fill in the required information, and save the file to your flash drive.

After completing this lab, you will be able to:

■ Create and configure a one-way external trust

■ Create and configure a two-way forest trust

■ Validate and test a trust

■ Configure selective authorization between two trusted domains

Estimated lab time: 80 minutes

Exercise 15.1	Creating and Configuring a One-Way External Trust
Overview	In this exercise, you will create a one-way external trust between the contoso.com domain and the adatum.com domain.
Mindset	Your company, contoso.com, has teamed up with another company, adatum.com. You want users from the adatum.com to access resources in the contoso.com domain. What should you do to allow this?
Completion time	25 minutes

1. Log in to RWDC01 as **contoso\administrator** with the password of **Pa$$w0rd**.

2. In Server Manager, click **Tools > DNS**.

3. In the DNS Manager console, right-click **Conditional Forwarders** and choose **New Conditional Forwarder**.

4. In the New Conditional Forwarder dialog box, in the DNS Domain text box, type **Adatum.com**.

5. Click **Click here to add** text, type **192.168.1.80** (as shown in Figure 15-1), and then press **Enter**. Click **OK**.

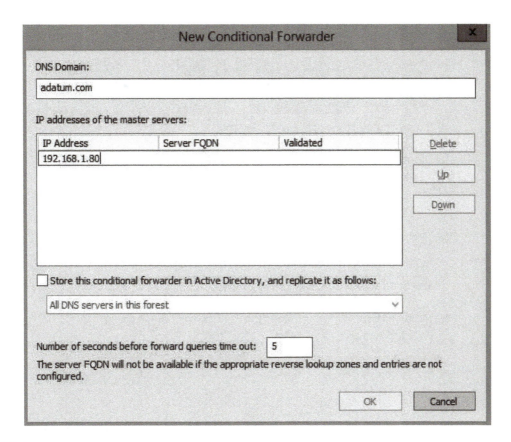

Figure 15-1
Creating a conditional forwarder zone

6. Close **DNS Manager**.

7. Log in to **Storage01** as **adatum\administrator** with the password of **Pa$$w0rd**.

8. In Server Manager, click **Tools > DNS**.

9. In the DNS Manager console, expand **Storage01**.

10. Right-click **Conditional Forwarders** and choose **New Conditional Forwarder**.

11. In the New Conditional Forwarder dialog box, in the DNS Domain text box, type **contoso.com**.

12. Click **Click here to add** text, type **192.168.1.50**, and then press **Enter**. Click **OK**.

13. Close **DNS Manager**.

14. On RWDC01, in **Server Manager**, click **Tools > Active Directory Domains and Trusts**.

15. On RWDC01, on the Active Directory Domains and Trusts page, right-click **contoso.com** and choose **Properties**.

16. In the Properties dialog box, click the **Trusts** tab (see Figure 15-2).

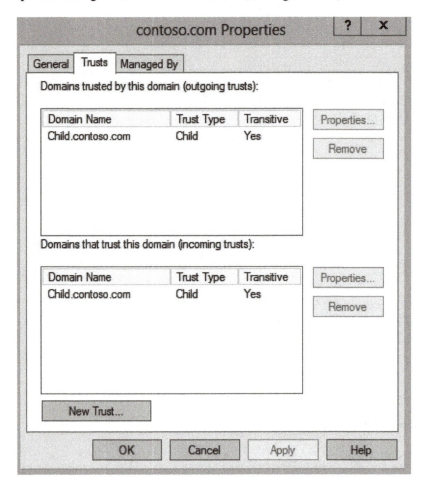

Figure 15-2
Opening the Trusts tab

Question 1	*What trust is already there and how was it created?*

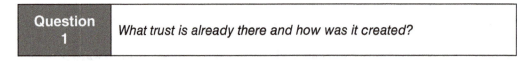

17. Click the **New Trust** button.

18. In the New Trust Wizard, click **Next**.

19. On the Trust Name page, in the Name text box (as shown in Figure 15-3), type **adatum.com** and then click **Next**.

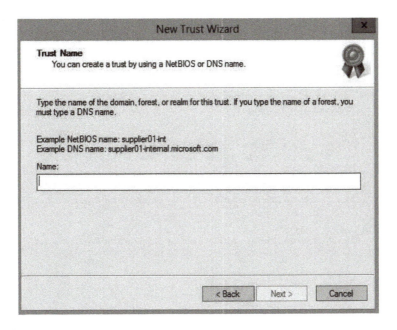

Figure 15-3
Defining the trust name

20. On the Trust Type page, External trust is already selected. Answer the next question and then click **Next**.

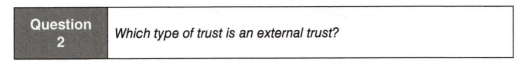

Question 2	Which type of trust is an external trust?

21. Select the **One-way: outgoing** option (see Figure 15-4) and then click **Next**.

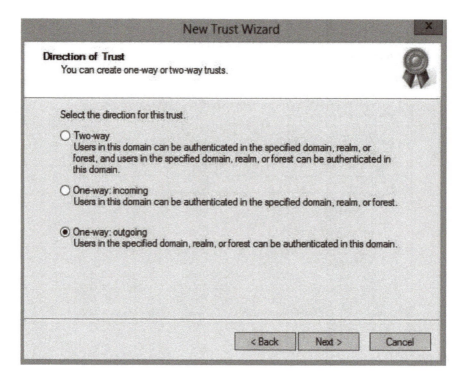

Figure 15-4
Specifying the direction of the trust

22. Select the **Both this domain and the specified domain** option and then click the **Next** button.

23. On the User Name and Password page, type the following:

    User name: **adatum\administrator**

    Password: **Pa$$w0rd**

24. Click **Next**, choose the **Domain-wide authentication** option, and then click **Next**.

25. The Trust Selections Complete prompt displays. Click **Next** to create the trust.

26. On success, this displays the Trust Creation Complete prompt. Click **Next**.

27. To confirm the trust, select the **Yes, confirm the outgoing trust** tab and then click **Next**.

28. Verify that the trust was successfully created and then click **Finish**.

29. In the SID Filtering information box, click **OK**. The adatum.com site appears in the outgoing trusts.

30. Take a screen shot of the contoso.com Properties dialog box by pressing Alt+Prt Scr and then paste it into your Lab 15 worksheet file in the page provided by pressing Ctrl+V.

31. Click **OK** to close the Properties dialog box.

End of exercise. Leave the Active Directory Domains and Trusts console open for the next exercise.

Exercise 15.2	Creating and Configuring a Two-Way Forest Trust
Overview	In this exercise, you will delete the trust you created in the last exercise and then create a two-way forest trust between contoso.com and adatum.com.
Mindset	
Completion time	20 minutes

1. On RWDC01, on the Active Directory Domains and Trusts page, right-click **contoso.com** and choose **Properties**.

2. In the Properties dialog box, click the **Trusts** tab.

3. Click **adatum.com** in the Domains trusted by this domain and then click **Remove**.

4. In the Active Directory Domain Services dialog box, click **Yes, remove the trust from both the local domain and the other domain**. Then specify the following information and click **OK**.

User name: **adatum\administrator**

Password: **Pa$$w0rd**

5. When you are prompted to confirm that you want to remove the outgoing trust, click **Yes**.

6. In the Properties dialog box, click the **New Trust** button.

7. In the New Trust Wizard, click **Next**.

8. On the Trust Name page, in the Name text box, type **adatum.com** and then click **Next**.

9. On the Trust Type page, click **Forest trust**. Answer the next question and then click **Next**.

Question 3	Which type of trusts is an external trust?

10. On the Direction of Trust page, select **Two-way** and then click **Next**.

11. On the Sides of Trust page, click **Both this domain and the selected domain** and then click **Next**.

12. On the User Name and Password page, type the following and then click **Next**:

    User name: **adatum\administrator**

    Password: **Pa$$w0rd**

13. On the Outgoing Trust Authentication Level-Local Forest page, click **Forest-wide authentication** and then click **Next**.

14. On the Outgoing Trust Authentication Level-Specified Forest page, click **Forest Wide authentication** and then click **Next**.

15. The Trust Selections Complete prompt displays. Click **Next**.

16. On the Routed Name Suffixes – Specified forest page (see Figure 15-5), click **Next**.

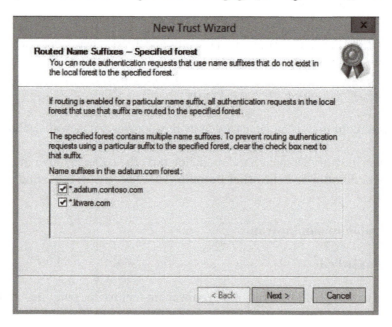

Figure 15-5
Specifying the routed name suffixes used in the trust

17. Once the trust is successfully created, the Trust Creation Complete prompt is displayed. Click **Next**.

18. On the Confirm Outgoing Trust page, to confirm the trust, click **Yes, confirm the outgoing trust** and then click **Next**.

19. On the Confirm Incoming Trust page, to confirm the trust, click **Yes, confirm the incoming trust** and then click **Next**.

20. When the wizard is complete, click **Finish**.

21. Take a screen shot of the contoso.com Properties dialog box by pressing Alt+Prt Scr and then paste it into your Lab 15 worksheet file in the page provided by pressing Ctrl+V.

22. Click **OK** to close the Properties dialog box.

End of exercise. Leave the Active Directory Domains and Trusts console open for the next exercise.

Exercise 15.3	Validating and Testing a Trust
Overview	In this exercise, you will validate a trust that you just created. In addition, you will access a shared folder from one domain to another domain using the trust.
Completion time	20 minutes

1. On RWDC01, on the Active Directory Domains and Trusts page, right-click **contoso.com** and choose **Properties**.

2. Right-click **contoso.com** and choose **Properties**.

3. In the Properties dialog box, click the **Trusts** tab.

4. Under Domains trusted by this domain (outgoing trusts), click **adatum.com** and then click **Properties**.

5. In the adatum.com Properties dialog box, click **Validate**.

6. In the Active Directory Domain Services dialog box, **click Yes, validate the incoming trust**.

7. Specify the following and then click **OK**.

Username: **adatum\administrator**

Password: **Pa$$w0rd**

8. Click **OK** again. When the Active Directory Domain Services dialog box appears, prompting you to update the name suffix routing for this trust, click **No**.

9. Take a screen shot of the adatum.com Properties window by pressing Alt+Prt Scr and then paste it into your Lab 15 worksheet file in the page provided by pressing Ctrl+V.

10. Click **OK** to close the adatum.com Properties dialog box.

11. Click **OK** to close the contoso.com Properties dialog box.

12. On RWDC01, click the **File Explorer** icon on the taskbar.

13. Create the **C:\Data** folder.

14. Create a text file in the C:\Data folder named **test.txt**.

15. Right-click the **Data** folder and choose **Properties**.

16. In the Properties dialog box, click the **Sharing** tab.

17. Click the **Advanced Sharing** button.

18. In the Advanced Sharing dialog box, click to select **Share this folder**.

19. Click the **Permissions** button.

20. In the Permissions dialog box, grant **Allow Full Control** to **Everyone**.

21. Click **OK** to close Permissions dialog box.

22. Click **OK** to close the Advanced Sharing dialog box.

23. On the Properties dialog box, click the **Security** tab.

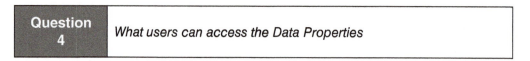

Question 4	*What users can access the Data Properties*

24. Click the **Edit** button.

25. In the Permissions dialog box, click **Add**.

26. In the Select Users, Computers, Service Accounts, or Groups dialog box, click the **Locations** button.

27. In the Locations dialog box (as shown as Figure 15-6), click **adatum.com** and then click **OK**.

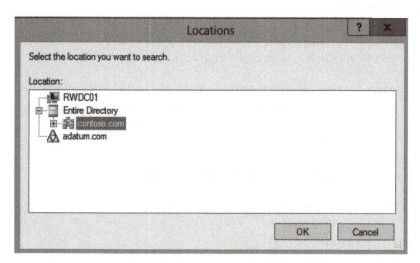

Figure 15-6
Selecting a domain when accessing remote resources

28. In the Enter the object names to select text box, type **domain users** and then click **OK** to close the dialog box.

29. Click **OK** to close the Permissions dialog box.

30. Click **Close** to close the Data Properties dialog box.

31. On Storage01, click the **File Explorer** button on the task bar.

32. In the Location box, type **\\rwdc01\data** (see Figure 15-7) and then press **Enter**. You should see the test.txt file.

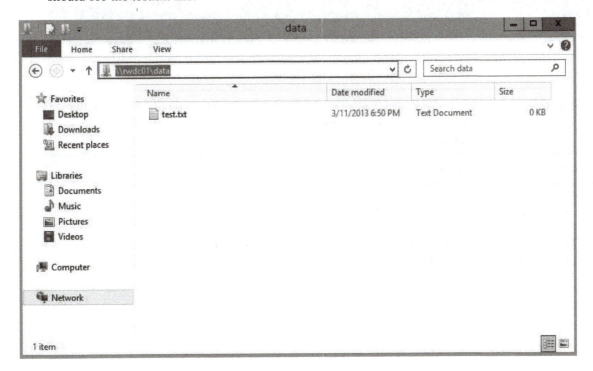

Figure 15-7
Accessing the \\rwdc01\data shared folder

33. Close **File Explorer**.

End of exercise. Close any open windows before you begin the next exercise.

LAB REVIEW QUESTIONS

Completion time   10 minutes

1. In Exercise 15.1, which tool did is used to create a trust relationship between two domains?

2. In Exercise 15.1, you need to define that a domain is trusted by another domain. Is this an outgoing trust or is this an incoming trust?

3. In Exercise 15.1, which type of trust is defined between a parent domain and a child domain?

4. In Exercise 15.2, which type of trust is created when you create a two-way forest trust?

5. There are three domains. Domain A trusts domain B, Domain B trusts Domain C. Therefore, Domain A trusts Domain C. Which type of trust is this?

6. In Exercise 15-3, how do you validate a trust between two domains?

Lab Challenge	Configuring Selective Authentication Between Two Trusted Domains
Overview	To complete this challenge, you will describe how to configure selective authentication between two trusted domains.
Mindset	Two domains (contoso.com and adatum.com) have an external share between the two domains. You want to configure selective authentication. What should you do?
Completion time	10 minutes

Write out the steps you performed to complete the challenge.

End of lab. You can log off or start a different lab. If you want to restart this lab, you'll need to click the End Lab button in order for the lab to be reset.

LAB 16
CONFIGURING SITES

THIS LAB CONTAINS THE FOLLOWING EXERCISES AND ACTIVITIES:

Exercise 16.1   Adding Sites and Subnets

Exercise 16.2   Configuring a Bridgehead Server

Exercise 16.3   Creating a Site Link

Exercise 16.4   Modifying the Replication Interval and Replication Schedule of a Site Link

Lab Challenge   Working with DNS SRV Records

BEFORE YOU BEGIN

The lab environment consists of student workstations connected to a local area network, along with a server that functions as the domain controller for a domain called contoso.com. The computers required for this lab are listed in Table 16-1.

Table 16-1
Computers required for Lab 16

Computer	Operating System	Computer Name
Server (VM 1)	Windows Server 2012 R2	RWDC01

In addition to the computers, you will also require the software listed in Table 16-2 to complete Lab 16.

Table 16-2
Software required for Lab 16

Software	Location
Lab 16 student worksheet	Lab16_worksheet.docx (provided by instructor)

Working with Lab Worksheets

Each lab in this manual requires that you answer questions, shoot screen shots, and perform other activities that you will document in a worksheet named for the lab, such as Lab16_worksheet.docx. You will find these worksheets on the book companion site. It is recommended that you use a USB flash drive to store your worksheets, so you can submit them to your instructor for review. As you perform the exercises in each lab, open the appropriate worksheet file, fill in the required information, and save the file to your flash drive.

After completing this lab, you will be able to:

- ■ Create and configure site and subnets

- ■ Configure a bridgehead server

- ■ Create a site link

- ■ Modify the replication interval and replication schedule of a site link

- ■ Manage registration of SRV records

Estimated lab time: 40 minutes

Exercise 16.1	Adding Sites and Subnets
Overview	In this exercise, you will add a site and a subnet to Active Directory. In addition, you will move a domain controller from one site to another site.
Mindset	Why is it important to define sites and subnets in Active Directory?
Completion time	15 minutes

1. Log in to RWDC01 as **contoso\administrator** with the password of **Pa$$w0rd**.

2. On RWDC01, when Server Manager, click **Tools > Active Directory Sites and Services**.

3. In the Active Directory Sites and Services console, expand the **Sites** folder.

Question 1	*What site is already created?*

4. Right-click the **Sites** folder and choose **New Site**.

5. In the New Object – Site dialog box, answer the following question.

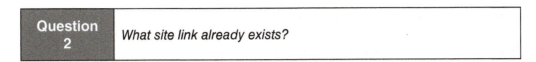

Question 2	*What site link already exists?*

6. In the Name text box, type **Corporate** and then click **DEFAULTIPSITELINK**. Click **OK**.

7. When the site has been created, answer the following question and then click **OK**.

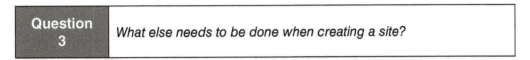

Question 3	*What else needs to be done when creating a site?*

8. Right-click the Subnets container and choose **New Subnet**.

9. In the New Object – Subnet dialog box (as shown in Figure 16-1), in the Prefix text box, type **192.168.1.0/24**.

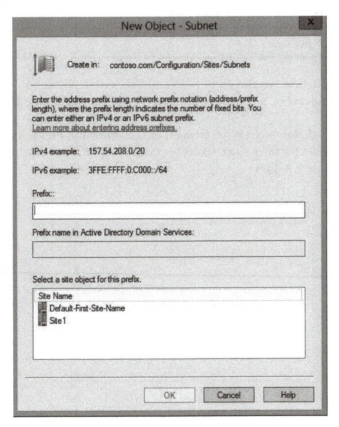

Figure 16-1
Creating a new subnet

10. Under Select a site object for this prefix, click **Corporate** and then click **OK**.

11. Expand **Subnets** and then confirm the **192.168.1.0/24** subnet is listed.

12. Expand **Default-First-Site-Name** and then expand **Servers**.

13. Right-click **RWDC01** and choose **Move**.

14. In the Move Server dialog box, click **Corporate** and then click **OK**.

15. Expand the **Corporate** site and then expand **Servers**. RWDC01 should be listed.

16. Take a screen shot of the Active Directory Sites and Services console by pressing **Alt+Prt Scr** and then paste it into your Lab 16 worksheet file in the page provided by pressing **Ctrl+V**.

Leave the Active Directory Sites and Services console open for the next exercise.

Exercise 16.2	Configuring a Bridgehead Server
Overview	In this exercise, you will create a bridgehead server.
Mindset	What is a bridgehead server and how can it make data replication more efficient?
Completion time	5 minutes

1. On RWDC01, using Active Directory Sites and Services, navigate to **Sites\Corporate\Servers**, and then right-click **RWDC01** and choose **Properties**.

2. On the Properties dialog box, on the General tab (as shown in Figure 16-2), under the Transports available for inter-site transfer section, click **IP** and then click **Add >>**. Click **SMTP** and then click **Add >>**.

Figure 16-2
Configuring a bridgehead server

3. Take a screen shot of RWDC01 Properties dialog box by pressing **Alt+Prt Scr** and then paste it into your Lab 16 worksheet file in the page provided by pressing **Ctrl+V**.

4. Click **OK** to close the Properties dialog box.

Leave the Active Directory Sites and Services console open for the next exercise.

Exercise 16.3	Creating a Site Link
Overview	In this exercise, you will create a site link.
Mindset	
Completion time	5 minutes

1. On RWDC01, using Active Directory Sites and Services, navigate to **Sites\Inter-Site Transports** and then right-click **IP** container and choose **New Site Link**.

2. In the New Object – Site Link dialog box, in the Name text box, type **SiteLinkBridge**.

3. As shown in Figure 16-3, Corporate and Default-First-Site-Name are already added to the Sites in this site link section. Click **OK**.

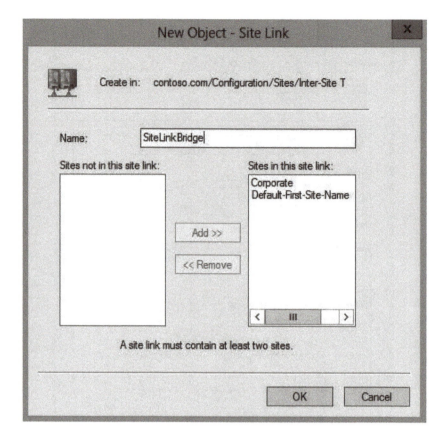

Figure 16-3
Creating a new site link

    4. Click the **IP** node.

    5. Take a screen shot of Active Directory Sites and Services console by pressing **Alt+Prt Scr** and then paste it into your Lab 16 worksheet file in the page provided by pressing **Ctrl+V**.

Leave the Active Directory Sites and Services console open for the next exercise.

Exercise 16.4	Modifying the Replication Interval and Replication Schedule of a Site Link
Overview	In this exercise, you will modify the replication interval and replication schedule of a site link.
Mindset	What can you use to force replication traffic to go over a particular site link when two sites have multiple site links connecting them?
Completion time	10 minutes

1. On RWDC01, using Active Directory Sites and Services, navigate to **Sites**, expand **\Inter-Site Transports**, and then click the **IP** folder.

Question 4	*The IP folder includes is DEFAULTIPSITELINK and SiteLinkBridge. What is the cost and replication interval of these two links?*

2. Right-click the **SiteLinkBridge** and choose **Properties**.

3. In the Properties dialog box, change the Replicate every setting to **60** minutes.

4. Click the **Change Schedule** button.

5. In the Schedule dialog box (as shown in Figure 16-4), click and drag from Monday 10 AM through Friday 2 PM and then click **Replication Not Available** (as shown in Figure 16-5).

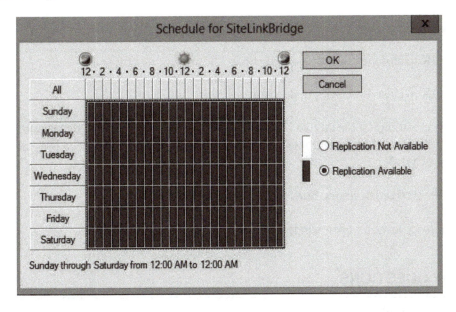

Figure 16-4
Showing the default scheduling

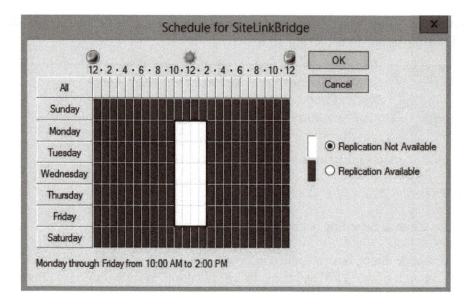

Figure 16-5
Changing the scheduling

6. Click **OK** to close the Schedule dialog box.

7. Click **OK** to close Properties dialog box.

8. Take a screen shot of the Active Directory Sites and Services console by pressing **Alt+Prt Scr** and then paste it into your Lab 16 worksheet file in the page provided by pressing **Ctrl+V**.

9. Close the **Active Directory Sites and Services** console.

End of exercise. Close any open windows before you begin the next exercise.

LAB REVIEW QUESTIONS

Completion time   5 minutes

1. In Exercise 16.1, what tool is used to create sites and subnets?

2. In Exercise 16.1, what tool is used to move domain controllers between sites?

3. In Exercise 16.2, what transport protocols are used by a bridgehead server?

Lab Challenge	Working with SRV Records
Overview	To complete this challenge, you will describe how to restore SRV records by writing the steps for the following scenario.
Mindset	You recently discovered that a junior admin deleted some of the SRV records, which caused some users to have problems logging in. What is the best way to re-create the SRV records?
Completion time	10 minutes

Write out the steps you performed to complete the challenge.

End of lab. You can log off or start a different lab. If you want to restart this lab, you'll need to click the End Lab button in order for the lab to be reset.

LAB 17
DESIGNING AN ACTIVE DIRECTORY PERMISSION MODEL

THIS LAB CONTAINS THE FOLLOWING EXERCISES AND ACTIVITIES:

Exercise 17.1   Planning an Active Directory Permission Model

Exercise 17.2   Customizing Tasks Using the Delegation of Control Wizard

Exercise 17.3   Delegating Permissions to AdminSDHolder

Exercise 17.4   Configuring Kerberos and Kerberos Delegation

Lab Challenge   Planning and Designing an Active Directory Permission Model
(Contoso Active Directory Permission Model Project)

BEFORE YOU BEGIN

The lab environment consists of student workstations connected to a local area network, along with a server that functions as the domain controller for a domain called contoso.com. The computers required for this lab are listed in Table 17-1.

Table 17-1
Computers required for Lab 17

Computer	Operating System	Computer Name
Server	Windows Server 2012 R2	CRWDC01

In addition to the computers, you will also need the software listed in Table 17-2 to complete Lab 17.

Table 17-2
Software required for Lab 17

Software	Location
Lab 17 student worksheet	Lab17_worksheet.docx (provided by instructor)

Working with Lab Worksheets

Each lab in this manual requires that you answer questions, shoot screen shots, and perform other activities that you will document in a worksheet named for the lab, such as Lab17_worksheet.docx. You will find these worksheets on the book companion site. It is recommended that you use a USB flash drive to store your worksheets, so you can submit them to your instructor for review. As you perform the exercises in each lab, open the appropriate worksheet file, fill in the required information, and then save the file to your flash drive.

SCENARIO

After completing this lab, you will be able to:

- Plan and design an Active Directory Permission Model

- Customize tasks using the Delegation of Control Wizard

- Delegate permissions to AdminSDHolder

- Configure Kerberos and Kerberos Delegation

- Plan and design an Active Directory Permission Model

Estimated lab time: 115 minutes

Exercise 17.1	Planning an Active Directory Permission Model
Overview	In this written exercise, you will read the background information for the Contoso Corporation provided in Appendix A, then read the information below, and then answer the questions.
Mindset	Active Directory consists of objects. Similar to NTFS permissions, Active Directory has permissions that specify what users can do with specified Active Directory objects.
Completion time	10 minutes

Question 1	*Is it rights or is it permissions that specify who can manage users and groups?*

Question 2	*You administer an organizational unit that contains all printers. What is the easiest way to assign a user so that the user can manage printers?*

Question 3	*How should you manage Active Directory users and computers from your Windows 8.1 machine?*

Question 4	*Which level should you assign a GPO that will configure Kerberos settings?*

Exercise 17.2	Customizing Tasks Using the Delegation of Control Wizard
Overview	In this exercise, you will create an OU and then delegate control of the OU.
Mindset	The Delegation of Control Wizard provides the easiest and most efficient way to assign permissions to an organizational unit so that the user or group can manage the organizational unit or perform some administrative function. By using the Delegation of Control Wizard, you can assign the minimum permission that the user or users need in order to complete their authorized tasks.
Completion time	15 minutes

1. Log in to CRWDC01 as **contoso\administrator** with the password of **Pa$$w0rd**.

2. On the CRWDC01, using Server Manager, open **Active Directory Users and Computers** console.

3. Right-click **contoso.com** and choose **New**. Then create the **Printer** OU.

4. Right-click the **Printer** OU and choose **New**. Then create a Global Security group named **PrinterAdmins**.

5. Right-click the **Printer** OU and choose **Delegate Control**.

6. In the Delegation of Control Wizard, on the Welcome screen, click **Next**.

7. On the Users or Groups page, click **Add**.

8. In the Select Users, Computers, or Groups dialog box, in the Enter the object names to select box, type **printadmin** and then click **OK**.

9. Back on the Users or Groups page, click **Next**.

10. On the Tasks to Delegate page, choose the following:

    ● **Create, delete, and manage user accounts.**
    ● **Create, delete, and manage groups**
    ● **Modify the membership of a group**

    Click **Next**.

Question 5	Which option should be chosen when you want the specified users to only manage computers?

11. When the wizard is complete, click **Finish**.

12. Right-click the **Printers** OU and choose **Properties**. Click the **Security** tab.

13. Click the **Advanced** button.

14. When the Advanced Security Settings for Printers opens, take a screen shot by pressing **Alt+Prt Scr** and then paste it into your Lab 17 worksheet file in the page provided by pressing **Ctrl+V**.

15. Click **OK** to close the Advanced Security Settings for Printers dialog box.

16. Click **OK** to close the Printers Properties dialog box.

Exercise 17.3	Delegating Permissions to AdminSDHolder
Overview	In this exercise, you will delegate permissions to AdminSDHolder using Active Directory users and Computers.
Mindset	The AdminSDHolder is used to secure privileged users and groups from unintentional modification. Every hour, the security permissions of the privileged group will be compared to the permissions listed in the AdminSDHolder object and reset them if they are different.
Completion time	15 minutes

1. On CRWDC01, log in using the **contoso\administrator** account and the **Pa$$w0rd** password.

2. Using Server Manager or Administrative Tools, open **Active Directory Users and Computers**. If needed, expand the **Contoso.com** node.

3. In the Users folder, in the **Users** OU, create an account named **SPAdmin**.

4. If you cannot see the System node, click **View > Advanced Features**.

5. Expand the **System** node.

6. Right-click **AdminSDHolder** and choose **Properties**.

7. In the **AdminSDHolder** Properties dialog box, click the **Security** tab.

8. Click the **Advanced** button.

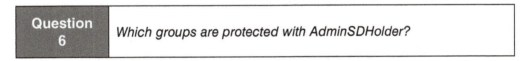

Question 6	Which groups are protected with AdminSDHolder?

9. Click the **Enable Inheritance** button and then click **Apply**. If you are prompted to continue, click **Yes**.

10. Click **Add**.

11. In the Permission Entry for AdminSDHolder dialog box, click the **Select a principal** link.

12. In the Select User, Computer, Service Account, or Group dialog box, in the Enter the object name to select, type **SPAdmin** and then click **OK**.

13. Under Permissions, select **Full Control** and then click **OK**.

14. Click **OK** to close the Advanced Security Settings for AdminSDHolder dialog box.

15. Take a screen shot of the AdminSDHolder Properties dialog box by pressing **Alt+Prt Scr** and then paste it into your Lab 17 worksheet file in the page provided by pressing **Ctrl+V**.

16. Click **OK** to close the AdminSDHolder Properties dialog box.

Exercise 17.4	Configuring Kerberos and Kerberos Delegation
Overview	In this exercise, you will create a Service Principal Name (SPN) for an account and then configure Kerberos delegation.
Mindset	An SPN is the name by which a client uniquely identifies an instance of a service. The client locates the service based on the SPN, which consists of three components: The service class, such as HTTP (which includes both the HTTP and HTTPS protocols) or SQLService; the host name; and the port (if port 80 is not being used).
Completion time	15 minutes

1. On CRWDC01, using Server Manager, click **Tools > ADSI Edit**. The ADSI Edit console opens.

2. Right-click **ADSI Edit** in the console tree and choose **Connect To**. In the Connection Settings dialog box, click **OK**.

3. Double-click Default Naming Context in the console tree, expand **DC=contoso,DC=com**, and then click **OU=Users**.

4. In the Details pane, right-click **CN=SPAdmin** and choose **Properties**. The CN=SPAdmin Properties dialog box opens.

5. In the Attributes list, double-click **servicePrincipalName** to display the Multi-valued String Editor dialog box.

6. In the Value to add field, type **http/portal.contoso.com:443** and then click **Add**.

7. Click **OK** twice.

8. Using Server Manager, click **Tools > Active Directory Users and Computers**.

9. Navigate to and click the **Users** organizational unit.

10. Right-click **SPAdmin** and choose **Properties**. The Properties dialog box opens.

11. Click the **Delegation** tab.

12. To allow this account to be delegated for a service, click **Trust this user for delegation to any service (Kerberos only)**.

13. Take a screen shot of the SPAdmin Properties Delegation tab by pressing **Alt+Prt Scr** and then paste it into your Lab 17 worksheet file in the page provided by pressing **Ctrl+V**.

Question 7	*How would you specify how long Kerberos tickets last?*

14. Click **OK**.

Lab Challenge	Planning and Designing an Active Directory Permission Model (Contoso Active Directory Permission Model Project)
Overview	In this written exercise, you will read the background information for the Contoso Corporation provided in Appendix A, then read the information below, and then write your plan.
Mindset	You are a new administrator for the Contoso Corporation, which is a leading company in producing smart devices for the home. You schedule a meeting with your manager to discuss tightening up Active Directory security. You are to develop a plan that outlines the company's Active Directory security policy.
Completion time	60 minutes

Create a proposal that includes the following sections:

- Purpose of the Project
- Requirements of the Project
- The Proposed Solution

When writing the proposal, you must explain the reasoning behind your choices.

End of lab. You can log off or start a different lab. If you want to restart this lab, you'll need to click the End Lab button in order for the lab to be reset.

LAB 18
IMPLEMENTING ACTIVE DIRECTORY FEDERATION SERVICES

THIS LAB CONTAINS THE FOLLOWING EXERCISES AND ACTIVITIES:

Exercise 18.1   Installing the Active Directory Federation Services

Exercise 18.2   Creating a standalone Federation Server

Exercise 18.3   Creating and Configuring a Sample WIF Application

Exercise 18.4   Implementing Relying Party Trusts

Exercise 18.5   Configuring the Active Directory Claims Provider Trust

Lab Challenge   Configuring a Global Authentication Policy

BEFORE YOU BEGIN

The lab environment consists of student workstations connected to a local area network, along with a server that functions as the domain controller for a domain called contoso.com. The computers required for this lab are listed in Table 18-1.

Table 18-1
Computers required for Lab 18

Computer	Operating System	Computer Name
Server (VM 1)	Windows Server 2012 R2	RWDC01
Server (VM 2)	Windows Server 2012 R2	Server01
Server (VM 3)	Windows Server 2012 R2	Server02

In addition to the computers, you will also require the software listed in Table 18-2 to complete Lab 18.

Table 18-2
Software required for Lab 18

Software	Location
Lab 18 student worksheet	Lab18_worksheet.docx (provided by instructor)

Working with Lab Worksheets

Each lab in this manual requires that you answer questions, shoot screen shots, and perform other activities that you will document in a worksheet named for the lab, such as Lab18_worksheet.docx. You will find these worksheets on the book companion site. It is recommended that you use a USB flash drive to store your worksheets, so you can submit them to your instructor for review. As you perform the exercises in each lab, open the appropriate worksheet file, fill in the required information, and save the file to your flash drive.

After completing this lab, you will be able to:

■ Install and configure Active Directory Federation Services

■ Configure Relying Party Trusts

■ Configure AD Claims Provider Trust Rules

■ Configure attribute store

Estimated lab time: 120 minutes

Exercise 18.1	Installing the Active Directory Federation Services
Overview	In this exercise, you will install Active Directory Federation Services.
Mindset	What is Active Directory Federation Services used for?
Completion time	15 minutes

1. Log in to Server01 as **contoso\administrator** with the password of **Pa$$w0rd**.

2. On Server01, in Server Manager, click **Manage > Add Roles and Features**. The Add Roles and Feature Wizard opens.

3. On the Before you begin page, click **Next**.

4. Select **Role-based or feature-based installation** and then click **Next**.

5. On the Select destination server page, click **Server01.contoso.com** and then click **Next**.

6. On the Select server roles page, click **Active Directory Federation Services** checkbox.

7. Click **Web Server (IIS)**. When you are prompted to add features, click **Add Features**.

8. Back on the Select server roles page, click **Next**.

9. On the Select features page, click **Next**.

10. On the Active Directory Federation Services (AD FS) page, click **Next**.

11. On the role services page, click **Next**.

12. On the Web Server Role (IIS) page, click **Next**.

13. On the Select role services page, click **Next**.

14. On the Confirm installation selections page, click **Install**.

15. When the installation is complete, take a screen shot of the Add Roles and Features Wizard by pressing **Alt+Prt Scr** and then paste it into your Lab 18 worksheet file in the page provided by pressing **Ctrl+V**.

16. Click **Close**.

End of exercise. Leave Server Manager open for the next exercise.

Exercise 18.2	Creating a Standalone Federation Server
Overview	In this exercise, you will first create a self-signed digital certificate using IIS. You will then use the AD FS Management to create a stand-alone federation server.
Mindset	
Completion time	10 minutes

1. On Server01, in Server Manager, click **Tools > Internet Information Services (IIS) Manager**.

2. In the Internet Information Services (IIS) Manager console, click **Server01**. If a message prompts you to get started with Microsoft Web Platform and stay connected with the latest Web Platform Components, click **No**.

3. Scroll down the middle pane and click **Server Certificates** (as shown in Figure 18-1). Double-click **Server Certificates**.

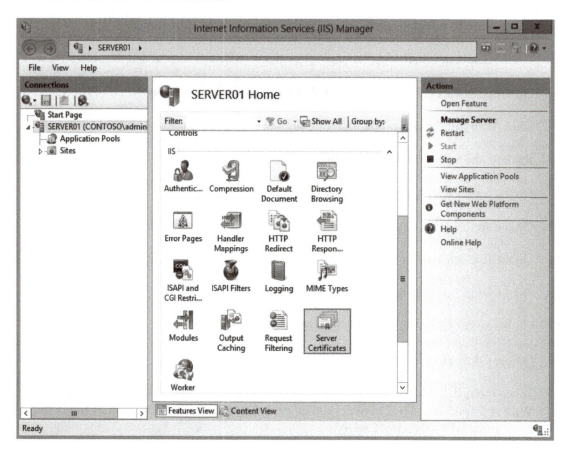

Figure 18-1
Opening Server certificates in IIS

4. Click **Create Self-Signed Certificate**.

5. On the Specify Friendly Name page, in the Specify a friendly name for the certificate text box, type **Server01.contoso.com**. Click **OK**.

6. Close **Internet Information Services (IIS) Manager**.

7. Click the **Windows PowerShell** button on the taskbar to open the Windows PowerShell window.

8. At the command prompt, execute the following command:

    Add-KdsRootKey–EffectiveTime (Get-Date).AddHours(-10)

9. Close the **Windows PowerShell** window.

10. In Server Manager, click the yellow triangle with the black exclamation point and then click **Configure the federation service on this server**.

11. On the Welcome page, the Create the first federation server in a federation server farm is already selected. Click **Next**.

12. On the Active Directory Domain Services page, click **Next**.

13. For the Specify Service Properties page, for the SSL Certificate, select **server01.contoso.com**. For the Federation Service Display name, type **Contoso Corporation**. Click **Next**.

14. On the Specify Service Account page, Create a Group Managed Service Account is already selected. For the Account name, specify **CONTOSO\ADFS**. Click **Next**.

15. On the Specify Configuration Database page, click **Next**.

16. On the Review Options page, click **Next**.

17. On the Pre-requisite Checks page, click **Configure**.

18. When the server has been configured, take a screen shot of the Results page by pressing **Alt+Prt Scr** and then paste it into your Lab 18 worksheet file in the page provided by pressing **Ctrl+V**.

19. Click **Close**.

20. Log in to RWDC01 as **contoso\administrator** with the password of **Pa$$w0rd**.

21. Right-click the **Start** button and choose **Command Prompt (Admin)**.

22. In the Administrator: Command Prompt window, execute the following command:

    setspn-S http/server01.contoso.com adfs

23. Close the **Administrator: Command Prompt** window.

24. On Server01, in Server Manager, click **Tools > AD FS Management**.

25. Take a screen shot of the AD FS console by pressing **Alt+Prt Scr** and then paste it into your Lab 18 worksheet file in the page provided by pressing **Ctrl+V**.

End of exercise. Leave the Server Manager open for the next exercise.

Exercise 18.3	Creating and Configuring a Sample WIF Application
Overview	In this exercise, you will install Windows Identity Foundation (WIF) SDK 4.0 so that you can install and configure a sample WIF application.
Mindset	
Completion time	40 minutes

1. Log in to Server02 as **contoso\administrator** with the password of **Pa$$w0rd**.

2. In Server Manager, click **Manage > Add Roles and Features**. The Add Roles and Feature Wizard opens.

3. On the Before you begin page, click **Next**.

4. Select **Role-based or feature-based installation** and then click **Next**.

5. On the Select destination server page, click **server02.contoso.com** and then click **Next**.

6. Click to select **Web Server (IIS)**. When you are prompted to add features, click **Add Features**.

7. Back on the Select server roles page, click **Next**.

8. On the Select features page, select the following:

   - **Expand .NET Framework 4.5 Features** and then select **ASP.NET 4.5**.

   - Select the **Windows Identity Foundation 3.5**.

Note	*At this time, be sure **not** to install .NET Framework 3.5. If you were to install .NET Framework 3.5, you would need to specify the location of Windows installation files so that the feature can be installed. If you select .NET Framework 3.5 and you do not specify the location of the Windows installation files, will cause the roles and features that are being installed at the same time to fail installation.*

9. On the Web Server Role (IIS) page, click **Next**.

10. On the Select role services page, make sure the following are installed:

    - Web Server (IIS)\Management Tools\IIS 6 Management Compatibility

    - Web Server (IIS)\Application Development\.NET Extensibility 4.5

    - Web Server (IIS)\Application Development\ASP.NET 4.5

When you are prompted to add features, click **Add Features**.

11. Click **Next**. On the Confirm installation selections page, click **Install**.

12. When the installation is complete, click **Close**.

13. To install the Windows Identity Foundation SDK, using File Explorer, navigate to **\\rwdc01\software** and double-click **WindowsIdentityFoundation-SDK-4.0.msi**. If you are prompted to confirm that you want to run this file, click **Run**.

14. In the Windows Identity Foundation SDK 4.0 Setup Wizard, click **Next**.

15. On the End-User License Agreement page, click to select **I accept the terms in the License Agreement** and then click **Next**.

16. On the Destination Folder page, click **Next**.

17. On the Ready to install Windows Identity Foundation SDK 4.0 page, click **Install**.

18. When the installation is complete, click **Finish**.

19. On the Welcome to the Microsoft Windows Identity Foundation page, you are prompted to set up Internet Explorer 11, click **Use Recommended security and compatibility settings** and then click **OK**.

20. Close the **Welcome to the Microsoft Windows Identity Foundation** window.

21. Close the **\\rwdc01\Software** folder.

22. In Server Manager, click **Tools > Internet Information Services (IIS) Manager**.

23. In Internet Information Services (IIS) Manager, click **Server02**.

24. In the Internet Information Services (IIS) Manager console, if a message displays, asking Do you want to get started with Microsoft Web Platform to stay connected with latest Web Platform Components prompt, click **No**.

25. Click and then double-click **Server Certificates**.

26. Click **Create Self-Signed Certificate**.

27. On the Specify Friendly Name page, in the Specify a friendly name for the certificate text box, type **Server02.contoso.com** and then click **OK**.

28. In the left pane, expand **Sites** and then click the **Default Web Site**.

29. Under Actions, in the Edit Site section, click **Bindings**.

Question 1	*What bindings are already defined?*

30. On the Site Bindings page, click **Add**.

31. In the Add Site Binding dialog box, change the Type to **https**. Then under SSL certificate, select **server02.contoso.com** (as shown in Figure 18-2) and then click **OK**.

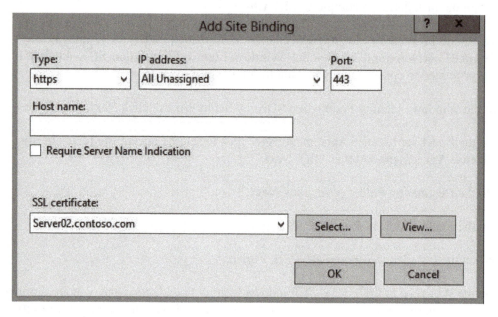

Figure 18-2
Binding a certificate to a website

32. Take a screen shot of the Site Bindings dialog box by pressing **Alt+Prt Scr** and choose paste it into your Lab 18 worksheet file in the page provided by pressing **Ctrl+V**.

33. Click **Close** to close the Site Bindings dialog box.

34. On the task bar, open File Explorer and then navigate to the **C:\Program Files (x86)\Windows Identity Foundation SDK\v4.0\Samples\Quick Start\Using Managed STS** folder.

35. Double-click **setup.bat**. Click **OK**. When the application has been created, press the spacebar.

36. Close the File Explorer window.

37. Click the **Start** button. In the Start menu, click the down arrow to show all programs and choose click **Windows Identity Foundation Federation Utility** (see Figure 18-3).

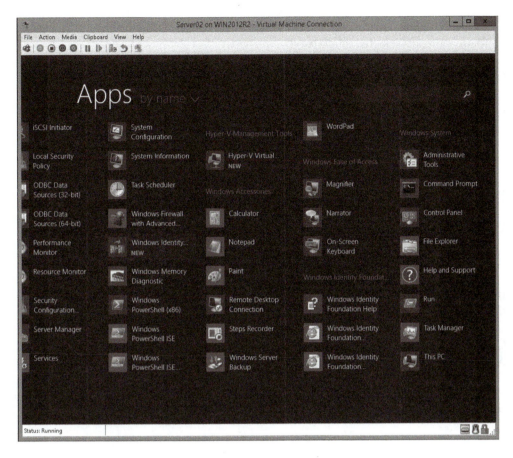

Figure 18-3
Accessing Windows Identity Utility from the Start menu

38. In the Federation Utility Wizard, in the Application configuration location text box, type the following:

C:\Program Files (x86)\Windows Identity Foundation SDK\v4.0\Samples\Quick Start\Using Managed STS\ClaimsAwareWebAppwithManagedSTS\web.config

39. In Application URI, type **https://server02.contoso.com/ClaimsAwareWebAppWithManagedSTS/** to indicate the path to the sample application that will trust the incoming claims from the federation server. Click **Next** to continue.

40. On the Security Token Service page, select **Use an existing STS**, type **https://server01.contoso.com/FederationMetadata/2007-06/FederationMetadata.xml** for the STS WS-Federation metadata document location text box and then click **Next** to continue.

41. When a warning displays, indicating that you are using a self-signed certificate, click **Yes**.

42. On the STS signing certificate chain validation error page, with Disable certificate chain validation already selected, click **Next**.

43. On the Security token encryption page, select **No encryption** and then click **Next**.

44. On the Offered claims page, review the claims that will be offered by the federation server and then click **Next**.

45. On the Summary page, click **Finish**.

46. When you have successfully configured the application, click **OK**.

47. Using Internet Information Services (IIS) Manager, click **Application Pools**.

48. In the Actions pane, click **Add Application Pool**.

49. In the Add Application Pool dialog box, in the Name text box, type **WIFSamples** and then click **OK**.

50. Click **WIFSamples** and, under Edit Application Pool in the Actions pane, click **Advanced Settings**.

51. Under Process Model/Generate Process Model Event Log Entry, change the Load User Profile setting from False to **True**, as shown in Figure 18-4.

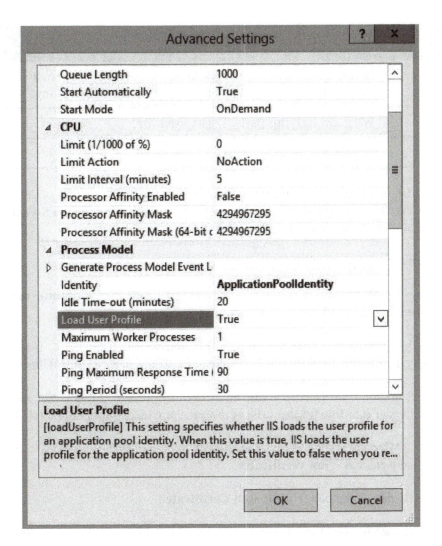

Figure 18-4
Modifying the application pool

52. Click **OK** to close the Advanced Settings dialog box.

53. In the left pane, expand **Sites**, expand **Default Web Site**, and then click **ClaimsAwareWebAppWithManagedSTS**.

54. In the Actions pane, click **Basic Settings**.

55. In the Edit Application dialog box, click **Select**.

56. In the Select Application Pool dialog box, change the Application pool to **WIFSamples** and then click **OK**.

57. Click **OK** to close the Edit Application dialog box.

End of exercise. Close any open windows before you begin the next exercise.

Exercise 18.4	Implementing Relying Party Trusts
Overview	In this exercise, you will implement a relying party trust so that the AD FS server knows what sites it will be supporting.
Mindset	What are Relying Party Trusts used for?
Completion time	20 minutes

1. On Server01, open Internet Explorer and then open the **https://server02.contoso.com/ClaimsAwareWebAppWithManagedSTS/FederationMetaData/2007-06/FederationMetadata.xml**.

2. If a security alert appears, click **OK**.

3. If you have a problem with the website's security certificate, click **Continue to this website (not recommended)**. If a security alert appears, click **OK**.

4. If a message appears, indicating the Content from the website listed below is being blocked by the Internet Explorer Enhanced Security Configuration, click **Close**.

5. Take a screen shot of the Internet Explorer window by pressing **Alt+Prt Scr** and then paste it into your Lab 18 worksheet file in the page provided by pressing **Ctrl+V**.

6. When the XML code is shown, click the white X in the red shieldlock at the top of the window and then click **View certificates**.

7. In the Certificate dialog box, click **Install Certificate**.

8. In the Certificate Import Wizard opens, click **Local machine** and then click **Next**.

9. On the Certificate Store page, click **Place all certificates in the following store** and then click **Browse**.

10. Click **Trusted Root Certification Authorities** and then click **OK**.

11. Back on the Certificate Store page, click **Next**.

12. When the wizard is complete, click **Finish**. When the import has been completed, click **OK**.

13. Click **OK** to close the Certificate dialog box.

14. Close **Internet Explorer** and then close all tabs.

15. On Server01, using the AD FS Management console, click **AD FS**, expand **Trust Relationships**, and then click **Relying Party Trusts**.

16. Right-click **Relying Party Trusts** (as shown in Figure 18-5) and choose **Add Relying Party Trust**.

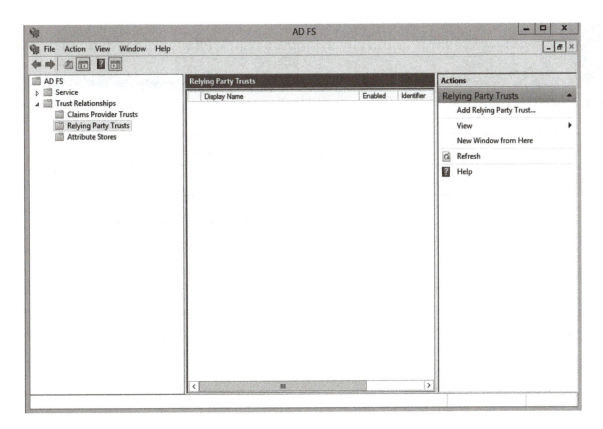

Figure 18-5
Viewing Relying Party Trusts

17. In the Add Relying Party Trust Wizard, click **Start**.

18. On the Select Data Source page, Import data about the relying party published online or on a local network is already selected. In the Federation metadata address (host name or URL) text box, type **https://server02.contoso.com/ClaimsAwareWebAppWithManagedSTS/** and then click **Next**.

19. On the Specify Display Name page, in the Display name text box, type **WIF Sample App** and then click **Next**.

20. On the Configure Multi-factor Authentication Now? page, click **Next**.

21. On the Choose Issuance Authorization Rules page, click **Permit all users to access this relying party** and then click **Next**.

22. On the Ready to Add Trust page, review the relying party trust settings and then click **Next** to save the configuration.

23. On the Finish page, click **Close** to exit the wizard.

24. Click **OK** to close the Edit Claim Rules for WIF Sample App.

End of exercise. Leave the AD FS console open for the next exercise.

Exercise 18.5	Configuring the Active Directory Claims Provider Trust
Overview	In this exercise, you will first create an claim rule. You will then test the WIF application.
Mindset	What does the claims provider trust identify?
Completion time	15 minutes

1. On Server01, in the AD FS console, under Trust Relationships, click **Claims Provider Trusts**.

Question 2	*What is the default claims provider trusts?*

2. In the middle pane, right-click **Active Directory** and choose **Edit Claim Rules**.

3. In the Edit Claims Rules for Active Directory window, on the Acceptance Transform Rules tab, click **Add Rule**.

4. In the Add Transform Claim Rule Wizard, in the Select Rule Template page, under Claim rule template, Send LDAP Attributes as Claims is already selected. Click **Next**.

5. On the Configure Rule page, in the Claim rule name box, type **Outbound LDAP Attributes Rule**.

6. In the Attribute Store drop-down list, select **Active Directory**.

7. In the Mapping of LDAP attributes to outgoing claim types section, select the following values for the LDAP Attribute and the Outgoing Claim Type (see Figure 18-6):

    •   **E-Mail-Addresses = E-Mail Address**

    •   **User-Principal-Name = UPN**

    •   **Display-Name = Name**

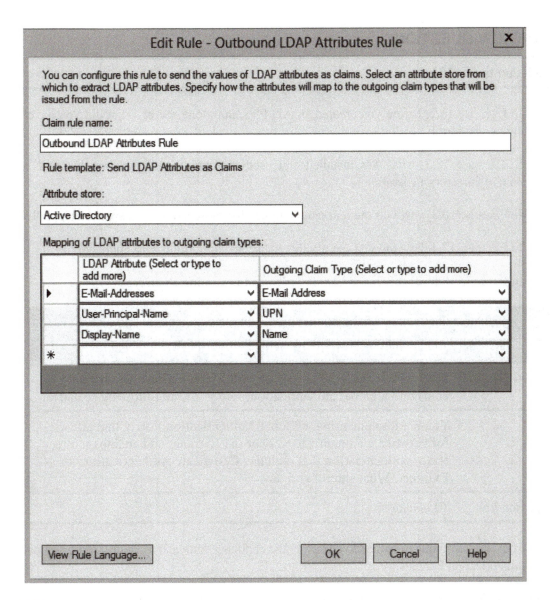

Figure 18-6
Editing a claim rule

8. Click **Finish** and then click **OK**.

9. Open Internet Explorer and open **https://server02.contoso.com/ClaimsAwareWebAppwithManagedSTS**. If a security alert displays, click **OK**.

10. When you are prompted to logon, log in as **contoso\administrator** using the password **Pa$$w0rd**. Click **OK**. If you an Internet Explorer dialog box appears, click **Close**. If a message appears, indicating a script is disabled, click **Submit**.

11. Take a screen shot of the resulting window by pressing **Alt+Prt Scr** and then paste it into your Lab 18 worksheet file in the page provided by pressing **Ctrl+V**.

End of exercise. Close any open windows before you begin the next exercise.

LAB REVIEW QUESTIONS

Completion time	10 minutes

1. In Exercise 18.2, before you created an AD FS stand-alone server, what did you have to create and install?

2. In Exercise 18.3, what was installed and used to supply an application that will use Active Directory Federation?

3. In Exercise 18.3, why was the federation application assigned its own application pool?

4. In Exercise 18.4, how did you specify the AD FS to support the WIF application?

5. In Exercise 18.5, what mapped LDAP attributes to outgoing claim types?

Lab Challenge	Configure a Global Authentication Policy
Overview	To complete this challenge, you will write the steps needed to configure a global authentication policy for the following scenario.
Mindset	You are implementing a Global Authentication Policy that allows for certificate authentication over the Extranet and enables multi-factor authentication that includes Certificate Authentication for Extranet. What should you do?
Completion time	10 minutes

Write out the steps you performed to complete the challenge and take a screenshot that shows the Authentication Policies.

End of lab. You can log off or start a different lab. If you want to restart this lab, you'll need to click the End Lab button in order for the lab to be reset.

LAB 19
INSTALLING AND CONFIGURING ACTIVE DIRECTORY CERTIFICATE SERVICES

THIS LAB CONTAINS THE FOLLOWING EXERCISES AND ACTIVITIES:

Exercise 19.1   Installing an Enterprise Certificate Authority

Exercise 19.2   Installing a Subordinate Certificate Server

Exercise 19.3   Configuring Certified Revocation List (CRL) Distribution

Exercise 19.4   Installing the Online Responder Role

Exercise 19.5   Performing a CA Backup

Lab Challenge   Managing Administrative Roles

BEFORE YOU BEGIN

The lab environment consists of student workstations connected to a local area network, along with a server that functions as the domain controller for a domain called contoso.com. The computers required for this lab are listed in Table 19-1.

Table 19-1
Computers required for Lab 19

Computer	Operating System	Computer Name
Server (VM 1)	Windows Server 2012 R2	RWDC01
Server (VM 2)	Windows Server 2012 R2	Server01

In addition to the computers, you will also require the software listed in Table 19-2 to complete Lab 19.

Table 19-2
Software required for Lab 19

Software	Location
Lab 19 student worksheet	Lab19_worksheet.docx (provided by instructor)

Working with Lab Worksheets

Each lab in this manual requires that you answer questions, shoot screen shots, and perform other activities that you will document in a worksheet named for the lab, such as Lab19_worksheet.docx. You will find these worksheets on the book companion site. It is recommended that you use a USB flash drive to store your worksheets, so you can submit them to your instructor for review. As you perform the exercises in each lab, open the appropriate worksheet file, fill in the required information, and save the file to your flash drive.

After completing this lab, you will be able to:

- Install an enterprise Certificate Authority

- Install a subordinate certificate server

- Configure a CRL distribution point

- Install and configure the Online Responder role

- Perform a CA backup

- Manage administrative roles

Estimated lab time: 110 minutes

Exercise 19.1	Installing an Enterprise Certificate Authority
Overview	In this exercise, you will install Certificate Authority and then configure the server as a root enterprise CA.
Mindset	What are the requirements to install an enterprise CA?
Completion time	20 minutes

1. Log in to RWDC01 as **contoso\administrator** with the password of **Pa$$w0rd**.

2. In Server Manager, click **Manage > Add Roles and Features**.

3. In the Add Roles and Features Wizard, click **Next**.

4. On the Select installation type page, click **Next**.

5. On the Select destination server page, click **Next**.

6. On the Select server roles page, select **Active Directory Certificate Services**. In the Add Roles and Features Wizard window, click **Add Features** and then click **Next**.

7. On the Select features page, click **Next**.

8. On the Active Directory Certificate Services page, click **Next**.

9. On the Select role services page, ensure that Certification Authority is selected and then click **Next**.

10. On the Confirm installation selections page, click **Install**.

11. On the Installation progress page, after installation is successful, click **Configure Active Directory Certificate Services on the destination server**, as shown in Figure 19-1.

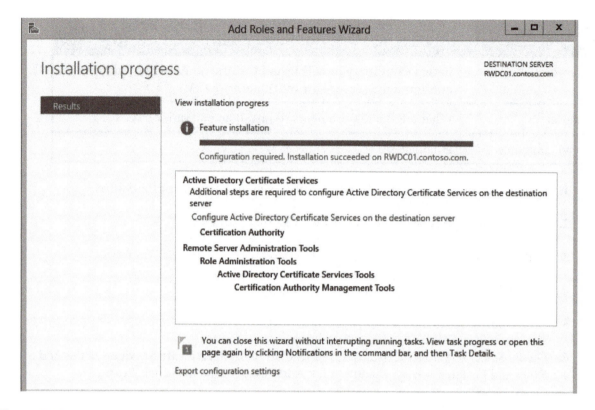

Figure 19-1
Configuring Active Directory Certificate Services after installation

12. On the Credentials page, click **Next**.

13. On the Select role services to configure page, click **Certification Authority** and then click **Next**.

14. On the Setup Type page, ensure that **Enterprise CA** is selected and then click **Next**.

15. On the CA Type page, ensure that **Root CA** is selected and then click **Next**.

16. On the Private Key page, ensure that Create a new private key is selected and then click **Next**.

17. On the Cryptography for CA page, answer the following question. Then change the Key length to **4096** and then click **Next**.

Question 1	What is the default key length?

18. On the CA Name page, answer the following question and then click **Next**.

Question 2	What is the default CA name?

19. On the Validity Period page, answer the following question, change the validity period to **10 years**, and then click **Next**.

Question 3	What is the default validity period?

20. The CA Database page displays where the certificate database will be stored. Answer the following question and then click **Next**.

Question 4	Where is the default database and log file location and why should caution be used here?

21. On the Confirmation page, click **Configure**.

22. Take a screen shot showing a successful configuration of the Active Directory Certificate Services by pressing **Alt+Prt Scr** and then paste it into your Lab 19 worksheet file in the page provided by pressing **Ctrl+V**.

23. Click **Close** to close the CA successful installation page.

24. Click **Close** to close the Add Roles and Features Wizard.

End of exercise. Close any open windows before you begin the next exercise.

Exercise 19.2	Installing Subordinate Certificate Server
Overview	In this exercise, you will install a subordinate certificate server, which will be under the root enterprise CA you created in the first exercise.
Mindset	What would determine how many subordinate CAs that an organization may need?
Completion time	20 minutes

1. Log in to Server01 as **contoso\administrator** with the password of **Pa$$w0rd**.

2. In Server Manager, click **Manage > Add Roles and Features**.

3. In the Add Roles and Features Wizard, click **Next**.

4. On the Select installation type page, click **Next**.

5. On the Select destination server page, select **Server01.contoso.com** and then click **Next**.

6. On the Select server roles page, select **Active Directory Certificate Services**. In the Add Roles and Features Wizard window, click **Add Features** and then click **Next**.

7. On the Select features page, click **Next**.

8. On the Active Directory Certificate Services page, click **Next**.

9. On the Select role services page, ensure that Certification Authority is selected and then click **Next**.

10. On the Confirm installation selections page, click **Install**.

11. On the Installation progress page, after installation is successful page, click **Configure Active Directory Certificate Services on the destination server**.

12. On the Credentials page, click **Next**.

13. On the Select role services to configure page, click **Certification Authority** and then click **Next**.

14. On the Setup Type page, select **Enterprise CA** and then click **Next**.

15. On the CA Type page, ensure that Subordinate CA is selected and then click **Next**.

16. On the Private Key page, ensure that Create a new private key is selected and then click **Next**.

17. On the Cryptography for CA page, keep the default selections for Cryptographic Service Provider (CSP) and Hash Algorithm. For better security, change the Key length to **4096** and then click **Next**.

18. On the CA Name page, click **Next**.

19. On the Certificate Request page, select **Send a certificate request to a parent CA**. Then with the CA name selected, click **Select**, click the CA that you installed in the previous exercise, and then click **OK**. See Figure 19-2. Click **Next**.

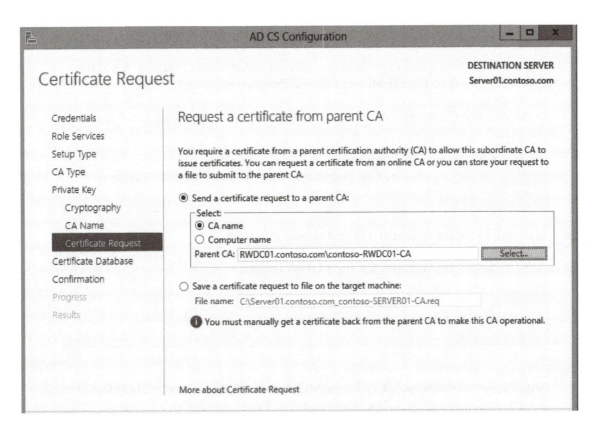

Figure 19-2
Requesting a certificate from the parent CA

20. The CA Database page displays where the certificate database will be stored. Click **Next**.

21. On the Confirmation page, click **Configure**.

22. Take a screen shot showing a successful configuration of the Active Directory Certificate Services by pressing **Alt+Prt Scr** and then paste it into your Lab 19 worksheet file in the page provided by pressing **Ctrl+V**.

23. Click **Close** to close the CA successful installation page.

24. Click **Close** to close the Add Roles and Features Wizard.

End of exercise. Leave Server Manager open for the next exercise.

Exercise 19.3	Configuring a Certified Revocation List (CRL) Distribution Point
Overview	In this exercise, you will configure a new Certified Revocation List (CRL) distribution point.
Mindset	What is a CRL?
Completion time	10 minutes

1. On Server01, in Server Manager, click **Tools > Certification Authority**.

2. In the Certification Authority console, double-click **contoso-Server01-CA** and then right-click **Revoked Certificates** and choose **Properties**.

3. In the Revoked Certificates Properties window, answer the following question and then click **OK**.

Question 5	What is the CRL publication interval and what is the Delta CRL publication interval?

4. Right-click **contoso-Server01-CA** and choose **Properties**.

5. In the Properties dialog box, click the **Extensions** tab.

Question 6	What are the four methods used to publish CRL?

6. Click the **http://<ServerDNSName>/CertEnroll/<CaName><CRLNAMESuffix><DeltaCRLAllowed>.crl** entry and then click **Remove**. Click **Yes** to confirm its removal.

7. To add additional CRL points, click **Add**.

8. In the Add Location dialog box, in the Location text box, type **http://**. Then select **<ServerDNSName>** from the Variable pull-down list and click **Insert**. So far, it should look like Figure 19-3.

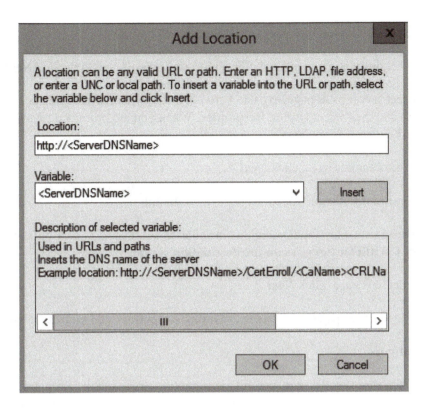

Figure 19-3
Specifying a new location for the CRL distribution

9. Add the necessary variables and text so that the Location is as follows:

   http://<ServerDNSName>/CertEnroll/<CaName><CRLNameSuffix><DeltaCRLAll owed>.crl

10. Click **OK** to close the Add Location dialog box.

11. Click **OK** to close the Properties dialog box. If you are prompted to restart the services now, click **Yes**.

End of exercise. Leave the Enterprise Certificate Authority console open for the next exercise.

Exercise 19.4	Installing the Online Responder Role
Overview	In this exercise, you will install and configure the Online Responder.
Mindset	How is an Online Responder more efficient than a CRL?
Completion time	35 minutes

1. On Server01, in Server Manager, click **Manage > Add Roles and Features**.

2. In the Add Roles and Feature Wizard, click **Next**.

3. On the Select installation type page, click **Next**.

4. On the Select destination page, click **Server01.contoso.com** and then click **Next**.

5. On the Select server roles page, expand **Active Directory Certificate Services (Installed)** and then select **Online Responder**. When you are prompted to add features, click **Add Features**. Click **Next**.

6. On the Select Features page, click **Next**.

7. On the Confirm installation selections page, click **Install**.

8. When a message displays, indicating that installation succeeded, click **Configure Active Directory Certificate Services on the destination server**.

9. In the Credentials page, click **Next**.

10. On the Role Services page, click to select **Online Responder** and then click **Next**.

11. Click **Configure**.

12. Take a screen shot showing a successful configuration of the Online Responder by pressing **Alt+Prt Scr** and then paste it into your Lab 19 worksheet file in the page provided by pressing **Ctrl+V**.

13. Click **Close** two times.

14. On Server01, using the Certification Authority console, right-click **contoso-Server01-CA** and choose **Properties**.

15. In the Properties dialog box, click the **Extensions** tab.

16. In the Select extension section, select **Authority Information Access (AIA)**, answer the following question, and then click **Add**.

Question 7	*What is the first entry for AIA?*

17. In the Add Location dialog box, specify **http://<ServerDNSName>/ocsp**, whereby <ServerDNSName> is a variable. Click **OK**.

18. Click to select the **Include in the AIA extension of issued certificates** check box.

19. Click to select the **Include in the online certificate status protocol (OCSP)** extension check box and then click **OK**.

20. When you are prompted to restart AD CS, click **Yes**.

21. In the certsrv console, under **contoso-Server01-CA**, right-click the **Certificate Templates** folder and choose **Manage**.

22. In the Certificate Templates console, double-click the **OCSP Response Signing** template.

23. In the OCSP Response Signing Properties dialog box, click the **Security** tab. Under Permissions for Authenticated Users, select the **Allow** check box for Enroll and Autoenroll and then click **OK**.

24. Close the **Certificate Templates** console.

25. In the Certification Authority console, right-click the **Certificate Templates** folder and choose **New > Certificate Template to Issue**.

26. In the Enable Certificate Templates dialog box, select the **OCSP Response Signing** template and then click **OK**.

27. Using Server Manager, click **Tools > Online Responder Management**.

28. In the ocsp console (as shown in Figure 19-4), right-click **Revocation Configuration** and choose **Add Revocation Configuration**.

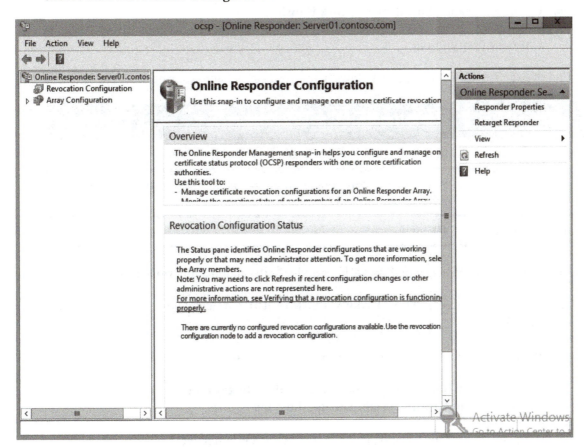

Figure 19-4
Viewing the ocsp console

29. In the Add Revocation Configuration Wizard, click **Next**.

30. On the Name the Revocation Configuration page, in the Name text box, type **Contoso CA Online Responder** and then click **Next**.

31. On the Select CA Certificate Location page, Select a certificate for an Existing enterprise CA option is already selected. Click **Next**.

32. On the Choose CA Certificate page, click **Browse**, click the **contoso-Server01-CA**, and then click **OK**. Then click **Next**.

33. On the Select Signing Certificate page, verify that Automatically select a signing certificate and Auto-Enroll for an OCSP signing certificate are both selected.

34. Take a screen shot of the Select Signing Certificate page by pressing **Alt+Prt Scr** and then paste it into your Lab 19 worksheet file in the page provided by pressing **Ctrl+V**.

35. Click **Next**.

36. On the Revocation Provider page, click **Finish**.

37. Close the ocsp console.

End of exercise. Close any open windows before you begin the next exercise.

Exercise 19.5	Performing a CA Backup
Overview	In this exercise, you will back up the certificate authority.
Mindset	What are the components that will need to be restored if you have to restore a CA?
Completion time	10 minutes

1. Using Server Manager on Server01, open the Certification Authority console.

2. In the console tree, right-click **contoso-SERVER01-CA** and choose **All Tasks > Back up CA**.

3. In the Certification Authority Backup Wizard, click **Next**.

4. On the Items to Back Up page, click to select **Private key and CA certificate**, and **Certificate database and certificate database log** options.

5. In the Back up to this location text box, type **C:\BAK**. Click **Next**.

6. On the Select a Password page, in the Password text box and the Confirm Password text box, type **Pa$$w0rd**. Click **Next**.

7. When the wizard is complete, click **Finish**.

8. Go to C:\BAK\ and confirm the CA has been backed up.

9. Open the **C:\BAK\DataBase** folder.

10. Take a screen shot of the DataBase folder by pressing **Alt+Prt Scr** and then paste it into your Lab 19 worksheet file in the page provided by pressing **Ctrl+V**.

End of exercise. Close any open windows before you begin the next exercise.

LAB REVIEW QUESTIONS

Completion time   10 minutes

1. In Exercise 19.1, how many enterprise root certificate authorities can you install for a domain?

2. In Exercise 19.2, how many subordinate CAs can you install for a domain?

3. In Exercise 19.3, what extension does the certificate revocation list have?

4. In Exercise 19.4, what is installed that has a similar functionality of CRL?

5. In Exercise 19.5, how did you perform a backup of the CA?

Lab Challenge	Managing Administrative Roles
Overview	To complete this challenge, you will describe how to manage Administrative Roles for Active Directory Certificate Services by writing the high-level steps for the following scenario.
Mindset	You installed a certificate authority for the Contoso Corporation and you need to define who will be the CA administrators and who will be the certificate managers. How do you assign these roles to your users?
Completion time	10 minutes

Write out the steps you performed to complete the challenge.

End of lab. You can log off or start a different lab. If you want to restart this lab, you'll need to click the End Lab button in order for the lab to be reset.

LAB 20
MANAGING CERTIFICATES

THIS LAB CONTAINS THE FOLLOWING EXERCISES AND ACTIVITIES:

Exercise 20.1   Importing and Exporting Digital Certificates

Exercise 20.2   Renewing a CA Certificate

Exercise 20.3   Creating a New User Certificate Template

Exercise 20.4   Requesting a Certificate

Exercise 20.5   Configuring Autoenrollment

Exercise 20.6   Configuring Enrollment Agents

Lab Challenge   Configuring the Key Recovery Agent

BEFORE YOU BEGIN

The lab environment consists of student workstations connected to a local area network, along with a server that functions as the domain controller for a domain called contoso.com. The computers required for this lab are listed in Table 20-1.

Table 20-1
Computers required for Lab 20

Computer	Operating System	Computer Name
Server (VM 1)	Windows Server 2012 R2	RWDC01
Server (VM 2)	Windows Server 2012 R2	Server01
Server (VM 3)	Windows Server 2012 R2	Server02

In addition to the computers, you will also require the software listed in Table 20-2 to complete Lab 20.

Table 20-2
Software required for Lab 20

Software	Location
Lab 20 student worksheet	Lab20_worksheet.docx (provided by instructor)

Working with Lab Worksheets

Each lab in this manual requires that you answer questions, shoot screen shots, and perform other activities that you will document in a worksheet named for the lab, such as Lab20_worksheet.docx. You will find these worksheets on the book companion site. It is recommended that you use a USB flash drive to store your worksheets, so you can submit them to your instructor for review. As you perform the exercises in each lab, open the appropriate worksheet file, fill in the required information, and save the file to your flash drive.

After completing this lab, you will be able to:

■ Manage certificate templates

■ Implement and manage certificate deployment

■ Manage certificate enrollment using Group Policies

■ Perform key recovery

Estimated lab time: 155 minutes

Exercise 20.1	Importing and Exporting Digital Certificates
Overview	In this exercise, you will export a digital certificate, delete the certificate that you exported, and then restore the certificate by importing the certificate.
Mindset	
Completion time	20 minutes

1. Log in to Server01 as **contoso\administrator** with the password of **Pa$$w0rd**.

2. On Server01, click the **Start** button, type **mmc**, and then press **Enter**. Click the mmc icon.

3. In the console, click File > **Add/Remove Snap-in**.

4. In the Add or Remove Snap-ins dialog box, double-click **Certificates**. On the Certificates snap-in dialog box, click **Computer account** and then click **Next**.

5. On the Select Computer dialog box, Local computer is already selected. Click **Finish**.

6. Back in the Add or Remove Snap-ins dialog box, click **OK**.

7. Under the Console Root, expand **Certificates,** expand **Personal**, and then click **Certificates** (below Personal).

8. Right-click **Server01.contoso.com** and choose **All Tasks > Export**.

9. In the Certificate Export Wizard, click **Next**.

10. On the Export Private key page, click **Yes, export the private key**. Click **Next**.

11. On the Export file format page, Personal Information Exchange –PKCS #12 (.PFX) is already selected. Click **Next**.

12. On the Security page, click to select **Password**. Then in the Password text box and the Confirm password text box, type **Pa$$w0rd**. Click **Next**.

13. On the File to Export page, type **c:\servercert.pfx** and then click **Next**.

14. When the wizard is complete, click **Finish**.

15. When the export is successful, click **OK**.

16. In the console, right-click **Server01.contoso.com** certificate that you just exported and choose **Delete**. When you are prompted to confirm that you want to delete this certificate, click **Yes**.

17. Open File Explorer by clicking the **File Explorer** icon on the task bar.

18. Navigate to the **C:** folder.

19. Double-click the **servercert** file.

20. In the Welcome to the Certificate Import Wizard, click **Local Machine** and then click **Next**.

21. On the File to Import page, click **Next**.

22. On the Private key protection page, in the Password text box, type **Pa$$w0rd**.

23. Click to select the **Mark this key as exportable** and then click **Next**.

24. On the Certificate Store page, click **Automatically select the certificate store based on the type of certificate** and then click **Next**.

25. When the wizard is complete, click **Finish**.

26. When the import is successful, click **OK**.

27. Back on the console, click **F5** to refresh the window. The Server01.contoso.com certificate should reappear.

28. Take a screen shot of the Certificates console by pressing **Alt+Prt Scr** and then paste it into your Lab 20 worksheet file in the page provided by pressing **Ctrl+V**.

29. Close the console. If you are prompted to save the console, click **No**.

End of exercise. Close any open windows before you begin the next exercise.

Exercise 20.2	Renewing a CA Certificate
Overview	If the digital certificate expires for the CA, digital certificates maintained by the CA also become invalid. Therefore, in this exercise, you will renew the digital certificate for the root and subordinate CA certificates.
Mindset	
Completion time	10 minutes

1. Log in to RWDC01 as **contoso\administrator** with the password of **Pa$$w0rd**.

2. On RWDC01, in Server Manager, click **Tools > Certification Authority**.

3. In the Certification Authority console, right-click **contoso-RWDC01-CA** and choose **All Tasks > Renew CA Certificate**.

4. When you are prompted to confirm that you want to stop Active Directory Certificate Services now, click **Yes**.

5. In the Renew CA Certificate dialog box, when you are prompted to confirm that you want to generate a new public and private key pair, click **No**. Click **OK**.

6. On Server01, in Server Manager, click **Tools > Certification Authority**.

7. In the Certification Authority console, right-click **contoso-RWDC01-CA** and choose **All Tasks > Renew CA Certificate**.

8. When you are prompted to confirm that you want to stop Active Directory Certificate Services now, click **Yes**.

9. In the Renew CA Certificate dialog box, when you are prompted to generate a new public and private key pair, click **No**. Click **OK**.

10. In the CA Certificate Request dialog box, click **OK**.

End of exercise. Leave the Certification Authority console open for the next exercise.

Exercise 20.3	Creating a New User Certificate Template
Overview	In this exercise, you will create a new user certificate and then make that certificate available to other users.
Mindset	
Completion time	20 minutes

Mindset Question: What permissions are required in order to request a certificate?

1. On Server01, using the Certification Authority console, expand **contoso-Server01-CA** and then right-click **Certificate Templates** and choose **Manage**.

Question 1	Which version is the User template?

2. In the Certificate Templates console, right-click the **User** template and choose **Duplicate Template**.

3. Click the **General** tab.

Question 2	What is the default validity period?

4. In the Template display name field, type **Corporate User Certificate**.

5. Click the **Subject Name** tab.

6. Clear the **Include e-mail name in the subject name** check box and clear the **E-mail name** check box.

7. Click the **Extensions** tab.

8. Click **Application Policies** and then click **Edit**.

9. In the Edit Application Policies Extension dialog box, click **Add**.

10. In the Add Application Policy dialog box, click **Smart Card Logon** and then click **OK** twice.

11. Click the **Superseded Templates** tab.

12. Click **Add**. Click the **User** template and then click **OK**.

13. Click the **Security** tab.

14. Click **Authenticated Users**, click **Allow Enroll**, and then click **Allow Autoenroll**.

15. Click **OK** to close the Properties of New Template dialog box.

16. Close the **Certification Templates** console.

17. Right-click **Certificate Templates** and choose **New > Certificate Template to Issue**.

18. In the Enable Certificate Templates window, select the **Corporate User Certificate** template and then click **OK**.

End of exercise. Close any open windows before you begin the next exercise.

Exercise 20.4	Requesting a Certificate
Overview	In this exercise, you will configure the web requests of certificate and then you will request certificates both manually and by using the web interface.
Mindset	What are the different ways to request a certificate?
Completion time	35 minutes

Installing Certification Installation Roles

1. On Server01, in Server Manager console, click **Manage > Add Roles and Features**.

2. In the Add Roles and Features Wizard, click **Next**.

3. On the Select installation type page, click **Next**.

4. On the Select destination server page, click **Server01.Contoso.com** and then click **Next**.

5. On the Select server roles page, expand **Active Directory Certificate Services (Installed)**, click to select the following, and then click **Next**:

    ● **Certificate Enrollment Policy Web Service**

    ● **Certificate Enrollment Web Service**

    ● **Certification Authority Web Enrollment**

    When you are prompted to add features, click **Add Features**.

6. On the Select features page, click **Next**.

7. On the Confirm installation selections page, click **Install**.

8. When the installation is complete, click **Configure Active Directory Certificate Services** on the destination server.

9. In the AD CS Configuration wizard, on the Credentials page, click **Next**.

10. On the Role Services page, click to select the following roles and then click **Next**:

    ● **Certification Authority Web Enrollment**

    ● **Certificate Enrollment Web Service**

    ● **Certificate Enrollment Policy Web Service**

11. On the CA for CES page, click **Next**.

12. On the Authentication Type for CES page, click **Next**.

13. On the Service Account for CES page, click **Use the built-in application pool identity** and click **Next**.

14. On the Authentication Type for CEP page, click **Next**.

15. On the Confirmation page, click **Configure**.

16. When the roles have been configured, take a screen shot of the AD CS Configuration page by pressing **Alt+Prt Scr** and then paste it into your Lab 20 worksheet file in the page provided by pressing **Ctrl+V**.

17. Click **Close**.

18. Click **Close** to close the Add Roles and Features Wizard.

Requesting a Certificate Using the Certificate Console

1. On Server01, click the **Start** button, type **mmc**, and then click the mmc icon.

2. In the console, click **File > Add/Remove Snap-in**.

3. In the Add or Remove Snap-ins dialog box, double-click **Certificates**.

4. In the Certificates snap-in dialog box, click **My user account**. Click **Finish**.

5. Back on the Add or Remove Snap-ins dialog box, click **OK**.

6. Under the Console Root, expand **Certificates** and then click **Personal**.

7. Right-click **Personal** and choose **All Tasks > Request New Certificate**.

8. In the Certificate Enrollment wizard, click **Next**.

9. On the Select Certificate Enrollment Policy page, click **Next**.

10. On the Request Certificates page, click to select the **Corporate User Certificate** option and then click **Enroll**.

11. When finished, click **Finish**.

12. Expand **Personal** and then click **Certificates**. You should see the Administrator user certificate. If you scroll over, you should also view the Certificate Type.

Requesting a Certificate Using the Web Interface

1. Open Internet Explorer and go to the following URL:

    https://server01.contoso.com/certsrv

    If a security alert appears, click **OK**.

2. When you are prompted to log in, log in as **contoso\administrator** with the password of **Pa$$w0rd**. Click **OK**.

3. In the Internet Explorer dialog box, click **Add**. On the Trusted sites box, click **Add**. Click **Close**.

4. On the Welcome page, click **Request a certificate**.

5. On the Advanced Certificate Request page, click **Create and submit a request to this CA**.

6. In the Web Access Confirmation dialog box, click **Yes**.

7. On the Advanced Certificate Request page, select the Corporate User Certificate in the Certificate Template section. At the bottom of the page, click **Submit**.

8. In the Web Access Confirmation dialog box, click **Yes**. In the Certificate Issued page, click **Install this certificate**.

9. Take a screen shot of the Internet Explorer window by pressing **Alt+Prt Scr** and then paste it into your Lab 20 worksheet file in the page provided by pressing **Ctrl+V**.

10. When the certificate has been installed, close **Internet Explorer**.

End of exercise. Close any open windows before you begin the next exercise.

Exercise 20.5	Configuring Auto-Enrollment
Overview	In this exercise, you will configure group policies to perform auto-enrollment of digital certificates.
Mindset	Which version of a digital certificate is required for auto-enrollment?
Completion time	10 minutes

1. On RWDC01, in Server Manager, click **Tools > Group Policy Management**.

2. In the Group Policy Management console, expand **Forest: Contoso.com**, expand **Domains**, expand **Contoso.com**, and then right-click **Default Domain Policy** and choose **Edit**.

3. In the Group Policy Management Editor, expand **User Configuration**, expand **Policies**, expand **Windows Settings**, expand **Security Settings**, and then click to highlight **Public Key Policies**.

4. In the right pane, double-click **Certificate Services Client – Auto-Enrollment**.

5. In the Configuration Model drop-down list box, click **Enabled**, as shown in Figure 20-1.

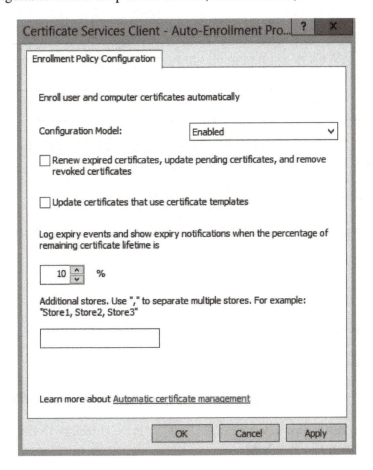

Figure 20-1
Enabling auto-enrollment

6. Click to select the **Renew expired certificates**, **Update pending certificates**, and **Remove revoked certificates** option.

7. Click to select the **Update certificates that use certificate templates** option.

8. Click **OK** to close the Properties dialog box.

9. In the right pane, double-click the **Certificate Services Client – Certificate Enrollment Policy** object.

10. On the Enrollment Policy tab, set the Configuration Model to **Enabled** and ensure that the certificate enrollment policy list displays the Active Directory Enrollment Policy.

11. Click **OK** to close the dialog box.

12. Close the Group Policy Management Editor and Group Policy Management console.

End of exercise. Close any open windows before you begin the next exercise.

Exercise 20.6	Configuring Enrollment Agents
Overview	In this exercise, you will configure enrollment agents, which can be used to create digital certificates for other users.
Mindset	What is a common reason that you would use an enrollment agent?
Completion time	30 minutes

1. On RWDC01, in Server Manager, click **Tools > Active Directory Users and Computers**.

2. Right-click the **Users** OU and choose **New > User**.

3. In the New Object – User dialog box, type the following and then click **Next**:

    First name: **Jay**

    Last name: **Bronze**

    Full name: **Jay Bronze**

    User logon name: **JBronze**

4. For the Password text box and then Confirm password text box, type **Pa$$w0rd**.

5. Click to select the Password never expires. In the Active Directory Domain Services dialog box, click **OK**. Click **Next**.

6. When done with the wizard, click **Finish**.

7. Right-click the Jay Bronze account in the Users OU and choose **Properties**.

8. Click the **Member of** tab.

9. Click **Add**. In the Select Groups dialog box, type **domain admins** and then click **OK**.

10. Click **OK** to close the Properties dialog box.

11. Close the Active Directory Users and Computers console.

12. On Server01, if the Certification Authority is not open, using Server Manager, click **Tools > Certification Authority**.

13. In the certsrv console, expand the **contoso-SERVER01-CA** and then right-click **Certificate Templates** and choose **Manage**.

14. In the Certificate Templates console, right-click **Enrollment Agent** and choose **Duplicate Template**.

15. Click the **General** tab.

16. For the Template display name, type **Corporate Enrollment Agent**.

17. Click the **Security** tab and then click **Add**.

18. In the Select Users, Computers, Service Accounts, or Groups window, type **Jay Bronze** and then click **OK**.

19. On the Security tab, click **Jay Bronze**, select **Allow Read** and **Allow Enroll** permissions, and then click **OK**.

20. Close the Certificate Templates console.

21. In the certsrv console, right-click **Certificate Templates** and choose **New > Certificate Template to Issue**.

22. In the list of templates, click **Corporate Enrollment Agent** and then click **OK**.

23. Log in to Server02 as **contoso\JBronze** with the password of **Pa$$w0rd**.

24. On Server02, click the **Start** button, type **mmc**, then click the mmc icon. If you a User Account Control dialog box appears, click **Yes**.

25. In Console1, click **File > Add/Remove Snap-in**.

26. Click **Certificates** and then click **Add**.

27. With **My user account** selected, click **Finish**.

28. Click **OK** to close Add or Remove Snap-ins.

29. Expand **Certificates – Current User**, expand **Personal**, and then click **Certificates**.

Question 3	*Jay Bronze has a digital certificate. Which template does the certificate use and how is the certificate created for Jay Bronze?*

30. Right-click **Certificates** and choose **All Tasks > Request New Certificate**.

31. In the Certificate Enrollment Wizard, click **Next**.

32. On the Select Certificate Enrollment Policy page, click **Next**.

33. On the Request Certificates page, select **Corporate Enrollment Agent** and then click **Enroll**.

34. When the certificate is installed, click **Finish**.

35. On Server01, in the Certification Authority console, right-click **contoso-SERVER01-CA** and choose **Properties**.

36. Click the **Enrollment Agents** tab.

37. Click **Restrict enrollment agents**.

38. When a warning displays, indicating that restrictions on delegated enrollment agents can be enforced only on Windows Server 2008 CAs or later, click **OK**.

39. In the Enrollment agents section, click **Add**.

40. In the Select User, Computer or Group field, type **JBronze**, click **Check Names**, and then click **OK**.

41. Click **Everyone** and then click **Remove**.

42. In the certificate templates section, click **Add**.

43. In the list of templates, click **Corporate User Certificate** and then click **OK**.

44. In the Certificate Templates section, click **<All>** and then click **Remove**.

45. In the Permission section, click **Add**.

46. In the Select User, Computer or Group field, type **domain admins**, click **Check Names**, and then click **OK**.

47. In the Permission section, click **Everyone** and then click **Remove**.

48. Click **OK** to close the Properties dialog box.

End of exercise. Close any open windows before you begin the next exercise.

LAB REVIEW QUESTIONS

Completion time   10 minutes

1. In Exercise 20.1,when exporting certificate, which format also exports the private key?

2. In Exercise 20.2, how do you ensure that a newer template will replace the older templates?

3. In Exercise 20.3, which methods can assign a digital certificate to a user?

4. In Exercise 20.4, what did you use to perform autoenrollment?

5. In Exercise 20.5, how did you make a user an enrollment agent?

Lab Challenge	Configuring the Key Recovery Agent
Overview	To complete this challenge, you will describe how to configure the Key Recovery Agent by writing the steps for the following scenario.
Mindset	You want to enable the Key Recovery Agent for the contoso.com domain. What are the primary steps for performing key archival and which tool is used to perform each step? Lastly, specify the steps necessary to recovering a certificate.
Completion time	10 minutes

Write out the steps you performed to complete the challenge.

End of lab. You can log off or start a different lab. If you want to restart this lab, you'll need to click the End Lab button in order for the lab to be reset.

LAB 21
INSTALLING AND CONFIGURING ACTIVE DIRECTORY RIGHTS MANAGEMENT SERVICES

THIS LAB CONTAINS THE FOLLOWING EXERCISES AND ACTIVITIES:

Exercise 21.1   Installing Active Directory Rights Management Service (AD RMS)

Exercise 21.2   Creating and Enabling the Super Users Group

Exercise 21.3   Creating a Distributed Rights Policy Template

Exercise 21.4   Enabling and Configuring an Application Exclusion

Lab Challenge   Backing Up and Restoring AD RMS

BEFORE YOU BEGIN

The lab environment consists of student workstations connected to a local area network, along with a server that functions as the domain controller for a domain called contoso.com. The computers required for this lab are listed in Table 21-1.

Table 21-1
Computers required for Lab 21

Computer	Operating System	Computer Name
Server (VM 1)	Windows Server 2012 R2	RWDC01
Server (VM 3)	Windows Server 2012 R2	Server02

In addition to the computers, you will also require the software listed in Table 21-2 to complete Lab 21.

Table 21-2
Software required for Lab 21

Software	Location
Lab 21 student worksheet	Lab21_worksheet.docx (provided by instructor)

Working with Lab Worksheets

Each lab in this manual requires that you answer questions, shoot screen shots, and perform other activities that you will document in a worksheet named for the lab, such as Lab21_worksheet.docx. You will find these worksheets on the book companion site. It is recommended that you use a USB flash drive to store your worksheets, so you can submit them to your instructor for review. As you perform the exercises in each lab, open the appropriate worksheet file, fill in the required information, and save the file to your flash drive.

After completing this lab, you will be able to:

- ■ Install and configure AD RMS

- ■ Create and enable the super users group

- ■ Create a distributed rights policy template

- ■ Enable and configure an application exclusion

- ■ Configure exclusion policies

- ■ Back up and restore AD RMS

Estimated lab time: 90 minutes

Exercise 21.1	Installing Active Directory Rights Management Services (AD RMS)
Overview	In this exercise, you will create the AD RMS service account, which will be needed when installing and configuring AD RMS. You will also define the RMS Users group and install the Active Directory Rights Management Service.
Mindset	
Completion time	40 minutes

1. Log in to RWDC01 as **contoso\administrator** with the password of **Pa$$w0rd**.

2. On RWDC01, in Server Manager, click **Tools > Active Directory Administrative Center**.

3. On the Active Directory Administrative Center, in the left pane, right-click **Contoso (local)** and choose **New > Organizational Unit**.

4. In the Create Organizational Unit dialog box, in the **Name** text box, type **Service Accounts** and then **OK**.

5. Click the little arrow next to **contoso (local)** to open a list of the top level OUs and then double-click the **Service Accounts** OU.

6. For the Service Accounts OU, under Tasks, click **New** and then click **User**.

7. In the Create User dialog box, configure the following options (as shown in Figure 21-1):

   First name: **ADRMS_SVC**

   User UPN logon: **ADRMS_SVC**

   Password and Confirm password: **Pa$$w0rd**

   Password options: **Other password options**

   Password never expires: **Enabled**

   User cannot change password: **Enabled**

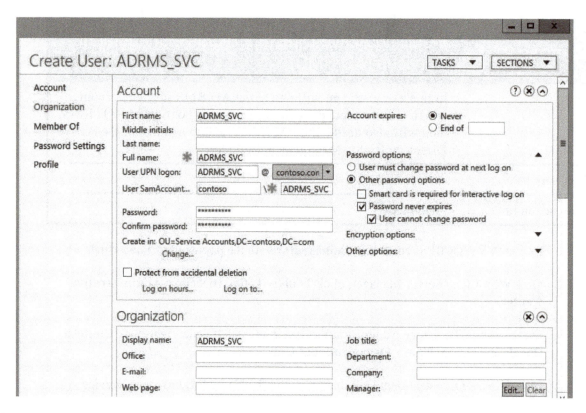

Figure 21-1
Creating an AD RMS service account

8. Click **OK** to close the Create User dialog box.

9. Click the small arrow next to **contoso (local)** and then double-click **Users**.

10. For the Users **OU**, under **Tasks**, click **New** and then click **User**.

11. In the Create User windows, type the following:

First name: **Thomas**

Last name: **Santes**

Full name: Thomas **Santes**

User UPN login: **TSantes**

Password and Confirm password: **Pa$$w0rd**

E-mail: **Thomas.Santes@contoso.com**

12. Under Password options, click **Other password options** and then click **Password never expires**.

13. Click **Member Of**.

14. Click **Add**.

15. In the Select Groups dialog box, in the Enter the object names to select text box, type **domain admins** and then click **OK**.

16. Click **OK** to close the Create User window.

17. For the Users OU, under Tasks, click **New** and then click **Group**.

18. In the Create Group dialog box, type the following:

    Group name: **RMS Users**

    E-mail: **RMSUsers@Contoso.com**

19. Scroll down to **Members**.

20. In the Members section, click **Add**. Type **Thomas Santes** and then click **OK**.

21. Click **OK** to close the Create Group dialog box.

22. Close **Active Directory Administrative Center**.

23. Using Server Manager, click **Tools > DNS**.

24. In DNS Manager, under RWDC01, expand the DNS server **Forward Lookup Zones** and then click **contoso.com**.

25. Right-click the **contoso.com** domain and choose **New Alias (CNAME)**.

26. In the New Resource Record dialog box, type the following:

    Alias name: **ADRMS**

    Fully qualified domain name (FQDN) for target host: **server02.contoso.com**

27. Click **OK** to close the New Resource Record dialog box.

28. Close **DNS Manager**.

29. Log in to Server02 as **contoso\administrator** with the password of **Pa$$w0rd**.

30. On Server02, in Server Manager, click **Manage** and then click **Add Roles and Features**.

31. In the Add Roles and Features Wizard, click **Next**.

32. On the Select installation type page, click **Next**.

33. On the Select destination server page, click **Server02.contoso.com** and then click **Next**.

34. Click to select **Active Directory Rights Management Services**. When you are prompted to add features, click **Add Features**.

35. On the Select server roles page, click **Next**.

36. On the Select features page, click **Next**.

37. On the Active Directory Rights Management Services page, click **Next**.

38. In the Select role services page, Active Directory Rights Management Server is already selected. Click **Next**.

39. On the Confirm installation selections page, click **Install**.

40. When the installation is complete, click **Close**.

41. Using Server Manager, click the **AD RMS** node.

42. At the top of the Servers section, next to Configuration required for Active Directory Rights Management Services at SERVER02 (as shown in Figure 21-2), click **More**.

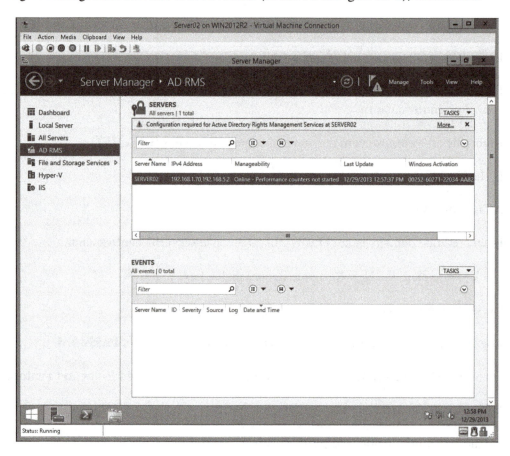

Figure 21-2
Configuring the AD RMS server

43. In the All Servers Task Details dialog box,, click **Perform additional configuration**.

44. In the AD RMS Configuration wizard, click **Next**.

45. On the AD RMS Cluster page, Create a new AD RMS root cluster is already selected. Click **Next**.

46. On the Configuration Database Server page, click **Use Windows Internal Database on this server**. Click **Next**.

47. On the Server Account page, click **Specify**.

48. In the Windows Security dialog box, type the following details, click **OK**, and then click **Next**:

- Username: **ADRMS_SVC**

- Password: **Pa$$w0rd**

49. On the Cryptographic Mode page, click **Cryptographic Mode 2** and then click **Next**.

50. On the Cluster Key Storage page, click **Use AD RMS centrally managed key storage** and then click **Next**.

51. On the Cluster Key Password page, in the Password text box and the Confirm Password text box, type **Pa$$w0rd** and then click **Next**.

52. On the Cluster Web Site page, verify that Default Web Site is selected and then click **Next**.

53. On the Cluster Address page, provide the following information and then click **Next**:

- Connection Type: **Use an unencrypted connection (http://)**

- Fully Qualified Domain Name: **adrms.contoso.com**

- Port: **80**

54. On the Licensor Certificate page, in the Name text box, type **ContosoADRMS** and then click **Next**.

55. On the SCP Registration page, click **Register the SCP now** and then click **Next**.

56. On the Confirmation page, take a screen shot of the Confirmation page by pressing **Alt+Prt Scr** and then paste it into your Lab 21 worksheet file in the page provided by pressing **Ctrl+V**.

57. Click **Install**.

58. When the installation is successful, click **Close**.

59. To manage AD RMS, you must sign out of Windows. Therefore, click **Start >
Administrator** and then click **Sign Out**.

End of exercise. Close any open windows before you begin the next exercise.

Exercise 21.2	Creating and Enabling the Super Users Group
Overview	In this exercise, you will create and enable the super users group.
Mindset	What is the Super Users group used for?
Completion time	15 minutes

1. On RWDC01, using Server Manager, click **Tools > Active Directory Administrative
Center**.

2. Click the **Users** OU. Under Tasks, click **New** and then click **Group**.

3. In the Create Group dialog box, type the following:

- Group name: **RMSSuperUsers**

- E-mail: **RMSSuperUsers@Contoso.com**

4. Under the Group scope section, select **Universal**.

5. Click **Members**.

6. Click **Add**. Type **domain admins; Thomas Santes** and then click **OK**.

7. Click **OK** to close the Create Group dialog box.

8. Close **Active Directory Administrative Center**.

9. Log in to Server02 as **contoso\administrator** with the password of **Pa$$w0rd**.

10. On Server02, in Server Manager, click **Tools > Active Directory Rights Management
Services**.

11. Take a screen shot of the Active Directory Rights Management Services window by
pressing **Alt+Prt Scr** and then paste it into your Lab 21 worksheet file in the page
provided by pressing **Ctrl+V**.

12. In the Active Directory Rights Management Services console, expand **server02 (Local)**
and then click **Security Policies**.

13. In the Security Policies area (as shown in Figure 21-3), under Super Users, click **Change
super user settings**.

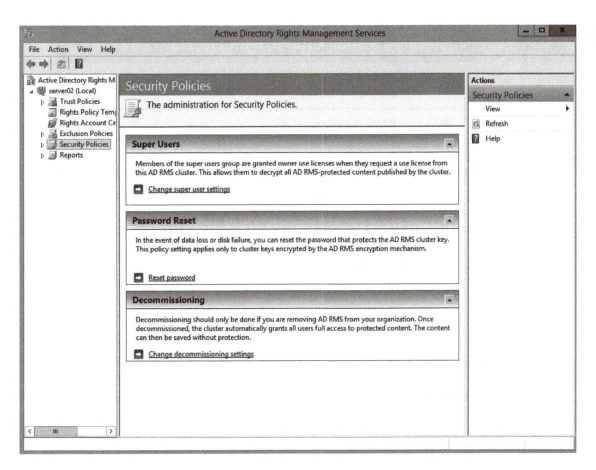

Figure 21-3
Changing super user settings

14. In the Actions pane, click **Enable Super Users**. The console shows Super users is enabled.

15. In the Super Users area, click **Change super user group**.

16. In the Super Users dialog box, click Browse. In the Select Group dialog box opens, type **RMSSuperUsers@contoso.com** and then click **OK**.

17. Click **OK** to close the Super Users dialog box.

18. Take a screen shot of the Super Users configuration by pressing **Alt+Prt Scr** and then paste it into your Lab 21 worksheet file in the page provided by pressing **Ctrl+V**.

End of exercise. Leave the Rights Management console open for the next exercise.

Exercise 21.3	Creating a Distributed Rights Policy Template
Overview	In this exercise, you will create a read-only distributed rights policy template.
Mindset	Why use RMS templates?
Completion time	10 minutes

1. On RWDC01, using Server Manager, open the Active Directory Administrative Center.

2. Click the Users **OU** and under **Tasks**, click **New** and then click **Group**.

3. In the Create Group windows, type the following:

   Group name: **Operations**

   E-mail: **Operations@contoso.com**

4. Click **Members**.

5. Click the **Add** button.

6. In the Select Users, Contacts, Computers, Service Accounts, or Groups dialog box, type **Thomas Santes** and then click **OK**.

7. To close the Create Group window, click **OK**.

8. On Server02, using the Active Directory Rights Management Services console, click **Rights Policy Templates**.

9. In the Actions pane, click **Create Distributed Rights Policy Template**.

10. In the Create Distributed Rights Policy Template Wizard, click **Add**.

11. On the Add New Template Identification Information page, type the following information and then click **Add**:

    ● Language: **English (United States)**

    ● Name: **Read-only template**

    ● Description: **Read only access. No copy or print**

12. Click **Next**.

13. On the Add User Rights page, click **Add**.

14. In the Add User or Group dialog box, type **operations@contoso.com** and then click **OK**.

15. When operations@contoso.com is selected, under the Rights section, click the **View** right. The Grant owner (author) full control right with no expiration is selected. Click **Next**.

16. On the Specify Expiration Policy page, choose the following settings and then click **Next**:

    - Content Expiration: Expires after the following duration (days): 7

    - Use license expiration: Expires after the following duration (days): 7

17. On the Specify Extended Policy page, click **Require a new use license every time content is consumed (disable client-side caching)** and then click Next.

18. On the Specify Revocation Policy page, click **Finish**.

19. Take a screen shot of the Distributed Rights Policy Templates by pressing **Alt+Prt Scr** and then paste it into your Lab 21 worksheet file in the page provided by pressing **Ctrl+V**.

End of exercise. Leave the Rights Management console open for the next exercise.

Exercise 21.4	Enabling and Configuring an Application Exclusion
Overview	In this exercise, you will create an exclusion policy that will specify which versions of PowerPoint documents to support.
Mindset	
Completion time	10 minutes

1. Under Server02 (Local) in the ADRMS console, click **Exclusion Policies** node.

2. Click **Manage application exclusion list** in the Application Exclusion pane.

3. In the Actions pane, click **Enable Application Exclusion**.

4. In the Actions pane, click **Exclude Application**.

5. In the Exclude Application dialog box, type the following information and then click **Finish**:

    - Application File name: **Powerpnt.exe**

    - Minimum version: **14.0.0.0**

    - Maximum version: **16.0.0.0**

6. To close the Exclude Application dialog box, click **Finish**.

7. Take a screen shot of the Application Exclusion by pressing **Alt+Prt Scr** and then paste it into your Lab 21 worksheet file in the page provided by pressing **Ctrl+V**.

End of exercise. Close any open windows before you begin the next exercise.

LAB REVIEW QUESTIONS

Completion time   5 minutes

1. In Exercise 21.1, what tool is used to configure AD RMS after it was installed?

2. In Exercise 21.2, how is a superuser group defined?

3. In Exercise 21.4, what is used to identify a group when you defined groups within an AD RMS template?

4. In Exercise 21.5, what is used to specify which version of an application will be supported by AD RMS?

Lab Challenge	Backing Up and Restoring AD RMS
Overview	To complete this challenge, you will explain how to back up and restore AD RMS for the following scenario.
Mindset	During the installation of AD RMS during this lab, you installed AD RMS with Windows Internal Database (WID). Explain the advantages of using a dedicated SQL server, particularly when looking at backing up and restoring AD RMS and how this back up affects the actual documents that are protected with AD RMS.
Completion time	10 minutes

Write out the steps you performed to complete the challenge.

End of lab. You can log off or start a different lab. If you want to restart this lab, you'll need to click the End Lab button in order for the lab to be reset.